PRAYING
BY THE
POWER OF
THE SPIRIT

Neil T. Anderson

HARVEST HOUSE PUBLISHERS

EUGENE, OREGON

PRAYING BY THE POWER OF THE SPIRIT
The Bondage Breaker® Series
Copyright © 2003 by Neil T. Anderson
Published by Harvest House Publishers
Eugene, Oregon 97402
www.harvesthousepublishers.com

Library of Congress Cataloging-in-Publication Data
 Anderson, Neil T., 1942–
   Praying by the power of the spirit / Neil T. Anderson.
     p. cm. — (The bondage breaker series)
   Includes bibliographical references.
   ISBN-13: 978-0-7369-1242-6
   ISBN-10: 0-7369-1242-8
   1. Prayer—Christianity. I. Title. II. Series.
   BV210.3.A53   2003
   248.3'2—dc21   2003001890

07 08 09 10 11 / VP-CF / 10 9 8 7 6

Contents

To my son, Karl, and his new wife, Rachel
You are beginning a new life together.
May the good Lord guide you, protect you, and meet all your needs
according to His eternal riches in glory.

Acknowledgments

For 60 years people have been building into my life. Books by authors I never met and tapes by people I never knew have contributed to my growth in Christ. I'm grateful for all the teachers that I have had over the years. I'm sure each one has contributed something to this book.

I want to thank Dr. Robert Saucy for reading through the rough draft and adding valuable insights to and making suggestions for the original manuscript. I have the highest respect for him because I know he loves the Lord and is committed to the truth.

I also want to thank my wife, Joanne. She has been my faithful companion who supports me and loves me enough to give me honest feedback.

I'm deeply grateful for Dr. Bill Bright and the staff of Campus Crusade for Christ. It was through their ministry that I found the Lord. Years later, I was one of the hundreds of people who dedicated their lives to full-time Christian ministry at Expo '72 in response to a message by Dr. Bright. (I was an aerospace engineer at the time.) It was Here's Life Publishers, a former ministry of Campus Crusade for Christ, that challenged me to put together the original manuscript of this book.

Finally, I want to thank all my friends at Harvest House. You make the process of writing easy, and your insights help me to be a better author.

Foreword

This is an excellent book that will be of help to the prayer life of every Christian. I found my own relationship with God being renewed as I read chapter after chapter. Neil Anderson brings together the teachings of the Bible and his own years of experience as a pastor, counselor, and professor, and the result is a wise, down-to-earth, balanced, and biblically sound book that corrects many misunderstandings about prayer and the Christian life.

I found the last chapter especially significant. After living more than 50 years as a Christian, and after teaching more than 25 years as a professor of Bible and theology, I took about two hours to work carefully through Neil's seven "Steps to Freedom in Christ" and apply each step to my own life, reading each suggested prayer aloud. God used that process to bring to mind a number of thoughts and attitudes that He wanted to correct, and then to impart to me a wonderfully refreshing sense of freedom, peace, joy, and fellowship with Himself.

Wayne Grudem, Ph.D.
Research Professor of Bible and Theology
Phoenix Seminary, Scottsdale, Arizona

CHAPTER ONE

Hearing from God

Prayer is not conquering God's reluctance but laying hold of God's willingness.

WHEN I WAS A NEW BELIEVER, I was told that prayer was a vital link in hearing God's voice. But prayer was also the most frustrating part of my early Christian experience.

As a seminary student, I read about the great saints who would spend two, three, or four hours a day in prayer—sometimes even all night. I was struggling to spend five minutes! I would labor through my prayer list for two or three minutes, then glance at my watch. Then I would try to figure out what I was going to say for the next two minutes. Prayer was supposed to be a dialogue with God, but most of the time it seemed like I was talking to the wall.

My greatest struggle was trying to stay focused. I had made a list of what I wanted to pray for, but distracting thoughts competed fiercely for my mind. Planned activities for the day were demanding my attention, and pesky thoughts would remind me of my many weaknesses. I spent a lot of time crucifying the flesh and rebuking Satan, assuming he was trying to distract me from my devotional life.

If prayer is so important, why is it so difficult?

My Struggles

In our Sunday school classes and small groups we arranged our chairs in little circles for prayer. If the second person to pray happened to be seated by the first person that prayed, a pattern was established. It seemed like an unwritten rule that each person would have to pray in turn as we went around the circle. If people didn't pray when it was "their turn," and you were supposed to follow them in the "established order," you would wonder what to do. *Why isn't she praying? Doesn't she know it's her turn? Maybe she's just gathering her thoughts. How long should I wait...or should I pass her by?*

When I was next in line to pray, I wasn't agreeing in prayer with the person praying. I was preoccupied with what I was going to say when it was my turn. Then someone would drone on and on, leaving nothing for the rest of us to pray for. They never got the message that long prayers are for the closet and short prayers are for the public.

As a young pastor, I also struggled with the pastoral prayer during the Sunday morning worship service. I became painfully aware I wasn't really praying to God, I was talking to the people. I was more conscious of the congregation's presence than I was of God's presence. I found myself summarizing the sermon or giving the week's announcements in the prayer. *Dear Lord, bless our church picnic next Saturday at 9 A.M. at the city park on the corner of Fifth and Central, and help us to remember that those with last names beginning with A through G are to bring salads....*That was no prayer—that was an announcement. Another member of the pastoral staff would drone on and on in King-James English. Was that more spiritual? (The teenagers would time him to see if he would break his 11-minute record!)

Realizing that prayer is an important part of any Christian marriage, my wife and I would spend time discussing what we needed to pray about. You would have overheard us saying to each other, "Let's pray about this...and we need to pray about that." After a lengthy discussion of what we thought we should pray about, we started to pray. We would go through the same list all over again, only this time we would address our prayers to God. I began to wonder where God was the first time we went through the list!

I know that God accepts our feeble efforts, but I sometimes wonder what He must be thinking. *There they go around the circle again! Why didn't that couple include Me in their initial discussion? Don't they know I'm omnipresent and omniscient?* I don't want to make fun of prayer, but where is the spiritual reality in our communication with God? What are we modeling when we pray publicly?

An Attitude of Gratitude

My prayer life turned the corner one evening when I was teaching a series of lessons on prayer to a group of college students. I was basing my messages on an old book about prayer. The last chapter was entitled "How to Pray in the Spirit." I read the first half of the book and thought it was theologically sound. So I advertised the titles of each chapter in the book to be the subjects of my lessons that summer. Not too creative, but typical of young pastors whose reservoir of wisdom is quite shallow. I didn't even read the last chapter of the book until the night before I was going to teach the college students how they were supposed to pray by the Spirit.

After reading that last chapter, I didn't have the foggiest idea how to pray by the Spirit (no reflection on the author of the book)! I was hours away from giving a message I had not incorporated into my own life. I felt spiritually bankrupt. If you have never been in such a spiritual state, then let me say that those times have the potential of being great moments with God!

I had all but given up trying to prepare a talk on how to pray by the Spirit and given in to plan B...which was to show a movie I had saved for such moments. Then came Jesus! It was approaching midnight when the Lord began to direct my thoughts. My journey through the Bible that evening turned out to be one of the most impactful experiences of my life. I began to reason, *If I'm going to pray in the Spirit, then I must be filled with the Spirit.* So I turned in my Bible to Ephesians 5:18-20:

> Do not get drunk with wine, for that is dissipation, but be filled with the Spirit, speaking to one another in psalms, and hymns and spiritual songs, singing and making melody in your heart to the Lord; always giving thanks for all things in the name of our Lord Jesus Christ, even the Father.

Then I turned to the parallel passage in Colossians 3:15-17:

> Let the peace of Christ rule in your hearts, to which indeed you were called in one body; and be thankful. Let the word of Christ richly dwell within you, with all wisdom teaching and admonishing one another with psalms and hymns and spiritual songs, singing with thankfulness in your hearts to God. Whatever you do in word or deed, do all in the name of the Lord Jesus, giving thanks through Him to God the Father.

As a seminary student, I had already observed that being "filled with the Spirit" and "letting the word of Christ richly dwell" within us had the same results. But I hadn't previously observed that both were connected to *giving thanks.* I turned a page in my Bible to Colossians 4:2: "Devote yourselves to prayer, keeping alert in it with an attitude of thanksgiving." Then I read Philippians 4:6: "Be anxious for nothing, but in everything by prayer and supplication with thanksgiving..." This discovery was getting me excited as I leafed over to 1 Thessalonians 5:17-18: "Pray without ceasing; in everything give thanks; for this is God's will for you in Christ Jesus."

Prayer and thanksgiving seemed to be inseparable. Like a little child finding another package under the Christmas tree—and another, and another—I started to examine Paul's own personal practices in his epistles, and this is what I found:

> I...do not cease giving thanks for you, while making mention of you in my prayers (Ephesians 1:15-16).

> I thank my God in all my remembrance of you, always offering prayer (Philippians 1:3-4).

> We give thanks to God, the Father of our Lord Jesus Christ, praying always for you (Colossians 1:3).

> We give thanks to God always for all of you, making mention of you in our prayers (1 Thessalonians 1:2).

> First of all, then, I urge that entreaties and prayers, petitions and thanksgivings, be made on behalf of all men (1 Timothy 2:1).

> I thank God, whom I serve with a clear conscience the way my forefathers did, as I constantly remember you in my prayers night and day (2 Timothy 1:3).

> I thank my God always, making mention of you in my prayers (Philemon 1:4).

I began to wonder if there was a connection between prayer and thanksgiving in the Old Testament. So the Lord reminded me of Psalm 95:

> O come, let us sing for joy to the LORD, let us shout joyfully to the rock of our salvation. Let us

come before His presence with thanksgiving. Let us shout joyfully to Him with psalms. For the LORD is a great God and a great King above all gods, in whose hands are the depths of the earth, the peaks of the mountains are His also. The sea is His, for it was He who made it, and His hands formed the dry land.

Come, let us worship and bow down, let us kneel before the LORD our Maker. For He is our God, and we are the people of His pasture and the sheep of His hand. Today, if you would hear His voice...(verses 1-7).

Hearing God's Voice

We should come before His presence with thanksgiving because He is a great God and He has done great things for us. We all deserved eternal damnation, but God has given us eternal life. That evening as I was reading the Scriptures, the seven last words in the above passage got my attention: "Today, if you would hear His voice." I remember thinking, *Today I would love to hear Your voice!* Maybe I wasn't hearing His voice because I wasn't coming before His presence with thanksgiving. Then again, maybe I wasn't hearing His voice because I wasn't really listening.

Many people in the Old Testament discovered the hard way that complaining does not bring God's blessings. In Psalm 95:7, the word *hear* is the Hebrew word *shema*, which means to "hear as to obey." Verse eight then reads, "Do not harden your hearts." I turned to Hebrews 4:7, which quotes Psalm 95, and read again, "Today if you hear His voice, do not harden your hearts." Hebrews chapter 4 gives instruction concerning the "Sabbath rest" that remains. It is an exhortation to cease trusting in our own works and begin to trust in God's works.

Resting in the finished work of Christ did not typify my prayer life. "In the name of Jesus" was just a phrase I tagged onto the end of my self-originated prayers. I confessed to God that my prayer time was mostly a work of the flesh, and that I didn't always come before Him with an attitude of praise and thanksgiving.

God-Directed Prayer

The Lord had a lot more for me that night. I turned to Romans 8:26-27:

> In the same way the Spirit also helps our weakness; for we do not know how to pray as we should, but the Spirit Himself intercedes for us with groanings too deep for words; and He who searches the hearts knows what the mind of the Spirit is, because He intercedes for the saints according to the will of God.

Humanly speaking, we really don't know how to pray or what to pray for, but the Holy Spirit does—and He will help us in our weakness. "Help" (*sunantilambano*) is a fascinating word in Greek. It has two prefixes in front of a word that is often translated as *take*. In other words, the sense of the word "helps" in Romans 8:26 is that the Holy Spirit comes alongside us, bears us up, and takes us over to the other side. The Holy Spirit connects us with God. He intercedes for us on our behalf. The prayer that the Holy Spirit prompts us to pray is the prayer that God the Father will always answer.

Active Listening

How does the Holy Spirit help us in our weakness? I wasn't sure, but I tried something that evening. I prayed, "Okay, Lord—I'm setting aside my list, and I'm going to assume that whatever comes to my mind during this time of prayer is from You or is allowed by You. I'm going to let You lead my time of prayer." Whatever came to my mind that evening was what I prayed about. If it was a tempting thought, I talked to God about that area of weakness. If the busyness of the day clamored for my attention, I discussed my plans with God. I actively dealt with whatever came to my mind.

I wasn't passively letting thoughts control me. I put up the shield of faith, which stands against Satan's flaming arrows, and I was actively "taking every thought captive to the obedience of Christ" (2 Corinthians 10:5). If you don't assume responsibility for your thoughts, you may end up paying attention to a deceiving spirit, as Paul warned us: "The Spirit clearly says that in later times some will abandon the faith and follow deceiving spirits and things taught by demons" (1 Timothy 4:1 NIV). Paul also wrote, "I am afraid that, as the serpent deceived Eve by his craftiness, your minds will be led astray from the simplicity and purity of devotion to Christ" (2 Corinthians 11:3).

If my thoughts weren't true or if they were evil (blasphemous, deceiving, accusing, or tempting), I didn't believe them. I brought those thoughts to the Lord and exposed them to the light of His Word. In one sense, it doesn't make any difference whether our thoughts come from an external source, or from our memories, or from a deceiving spirit, we are responsible to take every thought captive to the obedience of Christ. That meant, if my thoughts were coming from Satan, God was allowing it. In my experience, this typically identifies an area of weakness or sin that I have not previously been honest with God about. In fact, God may allow us to get buffeted around by Satan until we bring our struggles before Him, the only One who can resolve them.

Being Honest with God

In the past, I would try to shove evil thoughts away... without much success. But when I began to bring them to the light, I was amazed how liberating that was. All the issues I had been trying to ignore during prayer were issues God wanted me to deal with. He wanted to make me aware of matters that were affecting our relationship. Now when I have tempting or accusing thoughts, I share them honestly with God and don't try to hide my human frailty.

If you try praying like this, you will soon discover how personal God really is. "Today if you would hear His voice," is followed by the warning, "Do not harden your heart." When a thought that's hard to face comes into your mind, you will be tempted to change the subject and go back to your old prayer list. But why do you think God is allowing you to struggle with those thoughts? There may be many personal issues that we feel uncomfortable sharing with God, but that is part of the deception we experience. After all, God already knows our thoughts (see Hebrews 4:12-13), so why not be honest with Him? If God were to prioritize our prayer list, He would begin with the personal issues that affect our relationship with Him.

Over a number of years, after explaining the above in seminary classes, I challenged hundreds of my students to take a walk around the campus with God for the remainder of the class period. That would usually give them around 45 minutes, which was far more time than most of them would spend in their daily devotions. I encouraged them to start by thanking God for all He had done for them. I suggested they take their Bibles and just read if nothing came to mind. I encouraged them to deal honestly with any issues that came to their minds. If nothing came to mind, I instructed them to reflect upon God's goodness and thank Him for what He had done for them.

Many students returned with great stories. Some said they had accomplished more in that 45 minutes than they ever had before in prayer. Some dealt with personal issues that they had never discussed with God previously. One Asian student said he knew for the first time that God was calling him to minister in China. Almost all found it to be a refreshing encounter with their loving heavenly Father.

For myself, as I began to practice this, I found new freedom just sitting in the presence of God. I didn't feel like I had to say anything or keep a one-sided conversation going. It was actually refreshing, and I could simply sit in silence for an hour or more. I also discovered that my prayer time didn't end when I got up to do something else. I was learning to pray without ceasing and to practice the presence of God. Since I rode my bicycle to church, I started to pray for the people who lived in the houses along the way. The omnipresent God was always with me, and I was becoming more aware of it.

God Desires an Intimate Relationship with Us

Fellowship with God is not an abstract theological concept—it is a living relationship. John wrote, "If we walk in the light as He Himself is in the light, we have fellowship with one another, and the blood of Jesus His Son cleanses us from all our sin" (1 John 1:7). Walking in the light does not mean moral perfection, because the next verse reads, "If we say that we have no sin, we are deceiving ourselves" (verse 8). Rather, walking in the light is living in conscious moral agreement with God.

Mature Christians live a confessional life. *Confession to God* literally means to *agree with God*. We don't confess our sins in order to be forgiven. We are forgiven because Christ died for our sins on the cross, and therefore we confess our sins in order to have an intimate relationship with God. In fact, what makes it possible to be this open with Him about our present moral condition is the fact that we already *are* His forgiven children. In the matter of confession, our eternal destiny is not at stake, but our daily victory is. We don't have to pretend with God, having a false hope that He will accept us in our hypocrisy. As His children, we already are accepted, so we are free to be honest with Him.

Why is it so difficult to be honest with God? He demonstrated His love for us when He sent Jesus to die in our place (Romans 5:8). His love and forgiveness are unconditional. However, God is our Father, and like any good parent, He doesn't appreciate grumbling, complaining children, especially since He sacrificed His only begotten Son for every one of them. He will not be interested in our prayer lists if we aren't trusting and obeying Him. He is not going to help us develop our own kingdoms when we are called to establish His kingdom! Those who seek to build His kingdom and who come before His presence with thanksgiving will find grace and mercy in time of need,

> for we do not have a high priest who cannot sympathize with our weaknesses, but One who has been tempted in all things as we are, yet without sin. Therefore let us draw near with confidence to the throne of grace, so that we may receive mercy and may find grace to help in the time of need (Hebrews 4:15-16).

> Let us draw near with a sincere heart in full assurance of faith, having our hearts sprinkled clean from an evil conscience (Hebrews 10:22).

QUESTIONS FOR THOUGHT AND DISCUSSION

1. List reasons why you find prayer difficult in your personal life, with your spouse, and in small groups or during ministry.

2. In Paul's life, what attitude always accompanied prayer?

3. Why does an attitude of gratitude open our hearts to hear God's voice?

4. What kind of prayers will God the Father always answer? Why is this encouraging?

5. Why should you take every thought captive to the obedience of Jesus Christ during times of prayer?

6. What is the potential danger of passively believing your thoughts (see 1 Timothy 4:1; 2 Corinthians 11:3)?

7. What happens to our prayer life when we fail to be honest with God?

8. Why can we be totally honest with our heavenly Father without feeling condemned by Him?

CHAPTER TWO

Finding Freedom Through Prayer

*Prayer is not an argument with God to persuade him
to move things our way, but an exercise by which we
are enabled by His Spirit to move ourselves His way.*

LEONARD RAVENHILL

W HEN I WAS STILL TEACHING AT Talbot School of Theology, a
pastor asked if I would counsel a member of his church who was
hearing voices and experiencing the consequences of many
unresolved conflicts. I told the pastor I wouldn't unless he came
in with this young man, because I could not assume responsibility to follow up with him.

The three-hour session could not have gone any better.
The young man left with no voices or distracting thoughts, and
the peace of God was now guarding his heart and his mind. The
pastor was pleased with the results, but was totally surprised at
the process.

Why? What had set this young man free was *his* prayers and
response to God, not *mine*. The pastor remarked, "What a trap I
have gotten myself into. People come to me every Sunday and ask
me to pray for them. Of course I pray for them like any good
pastor would, but what I have overlooked is the individual
person's responsibility to pray."

If a hurting person asks someone else to pray, and that is all that happens, how many great answers to prayer result from that? I'll be honest with you—I haven't seen very many. I believe there is a very good reason for this…and it has little to do with my calling, level of maturity, or giftedness.

Our Responsibility in Prayer

There is only one passage in the Bible that definitively tells us what to do if we are sick or suffering, and that is James 5:13-18. Notice how this passage begins: "Is anyone among you suffering? Then he must pray." At least initially in the helping process, the one who is suffering is supposed to be praying. That has to happen because I cannot do your praying for you, nor can anyone else. Don't get me wrong—I believe in intercessory prayer, but not as a replacement for an individual's responsibility to pray.

When I first started to help people resolve their personal and spiritual conflicts and appropriate their freedom in Christ, more often than not I would get stuck in the process. I wouldn't know the cause of their problem, but I did know that God did and that ultimately He was the answer. Over the years, I have told many counselees that I don't know how to help them, but God does, and if they are willing, we will search together for God's answer. However, it used to be my practice to pray and ask God for wisdom for the other person, because James wrote, "If any of you lacks wisdom, let him ask of God, who gives to all generously and without reproach, and it will be given" (1:5).

I remember sitting with one person in silence for about 15 minutes, waiting for God's guidance. Then one day it dawned on me: *Why should I ask God for wisdom and direction on behalf of another person and then expect Him to tell me what the answer is? Why don't I encourage* them *to ask God for wisdom and direction?* The above passage in James says nothing about asking God for wisdom through another person. The instruction is that all believers should ask God for themselves. These people I was trying to help were God's children, and they all had the same access to their heavenly Father that I have.

Paul declared, "There is one God, and one mediator also between God and men, the man Christ Jesus" (1 Timothy 2:5). Christians are never instructed to function as mediums, like New Age channelers do. I know of no New Testament passage that instructs one believer to inquire of God on behalf of other believers who are in your presence. (There are many passages that teach *intercessory* prayer, of course, and we'll look at that issue in the next chapter.)

Children of God are invited to seek God themselves. To illustrate, suppose you have two sons—and the younger son keeps asking his older brother to make requests of you on his behalf. "Would you ask Dad if I can go to the movies?" "Would you ask Dad if I can have some money?" If you were a good father, what would you say to your older son? Wouldn't you say something like this: "Go tell your younger brother that he needs to come see me himself"? There are no such things as meaningful secondhand relationships, and there are certainly none in the family of God. Every born-again believer has a personal relationship with his or her heavenly Father.

Confidence to Enter God's Presence

Why do some people in the church believe that others have greater access to God than they do? Such thinking could be a holdover from pre-Reformation Catholicism. People were actually encouraged to pay someone of higher ecclesiastical position or maturity to pray for them. A further indication of this attitude was the sale of *indulgences,* through which, supposedly, the superabundant merit of the "saints" would compensate for the inadequate merit of the lowly individual. Martin Luther opposed the sale of indulgences and taught the priesthood of every believer.

Children of God are by definition *saints*. There are, however, some Catholic priests and Protestant clergy who think, or allow their people to believe, that they have greater access to the Father and their prayers are more efficacious because of their position in the church, their social standing, or their giftedness. But according to Paul, we *all* "have boldness and confident access through faith in Him" (Ephesians 3:12). The writer of Hebrews admonished *all* believers to draw near:

> Brethren, since we have confidence to enter the holy place by the blood of Jesus, by a new and living way which He inaugurated for us through the veil, that is, His flesh, and since we have a great priest over the house of God, let us draw near with a sincere heart in full assurance of faith, having our hearts sprinkled clean from an evil conscience and our bodies washed with pure water (10:19-22).

Connecting with God Through Repentance

For some people it is not an ecclesiastical issue but a moral one. Because of their lifestyle or deeds, they don't think God will hear them or answer their prayers. So they ask someone to pray for them, thinking that God will answer the other person's prayers. Actually, they are partly right. The psalmist wrote, "If I regard iniquity in my heart, the LORD will not hear me" (Psalm 66:18 KJV). As long as such people hang on to their sin and bitterness, they will not have an effective prayer life. But trying to get around their sin by asking someone else to do their praying for them will not work. The only effective prayer for this person is a prayer from their own repentant heart.

Understanding this simple concept about prayer revolutionized my ministry as a pastor. I used to listen to people's stories, try to explain why they weren't doing well (if I thought I knew), and encourage them to confess and repent if they were sinning.

Sometimes people would be asking only for biblical advice, and I would try to give it to them. I wasn't seeing much fruit, however, because I was usually treating just the symptoms and not getting to the root causes.

In those days I didn't understand the battle that was going on for their minds. I knew a little bit about helping those I was counseling to submit to God, but not enough to help them fully repent and resist the devil (James 4:7). I had a little knowledge about them—but God knew them perfectly. I could do my best to help them—but God was their Source of life, their Redeemer, Savior, Lord, and Friend. Somehow I had to connect them with God, or else they would never realize their freedom and full potential in Christ.

People don't know how to get out of bondage, or they would have a long time ago. And they don't know how or what to pray for in regard to their walk with God. Back then, my prayers certainly weren't setting them free, so I asked myself how I could help *them* pray in such a way that God would answer them. I can still remember that spring afternoon in 1984 when I wrote out seven specific prayers for people who were seeking to resolve their personal and spiritual conflicts. Those prayers have been modified over the years, but they still serve as the basis for the "Steps to Freedom in Christ," which are being used all over the world in many languages.[1] As people go through the Steps, what they are actually doing is petitioning God to reveal to their minds whatever is keeping them from having an intimate relationship with Him. In other words, they are asking God to grant them repentance leading to a knowledge of the truth so that they may escape the snare of the devil (see 2 Timothy 2:24-26).

Seven Areas of Confession and Repentance

Scripture reveals seven categories of sins and iniquities that need to be confessed and repented of if a Christian hopes to have an intimate relationship with God. Through the Steps, believers petition God to show them what they need to repent of in each of these areas.

First, *we should confess and renounce any involvement with false prophets and teachers, as well as any involvement with cults or the occult.* "He who conceals his sins does not prosper, but whoever confesses and renounces them finds mercy" (Proverbs 28:13 NIV). God does not take false teachers and false guidance lightly. In the Old Testament, false teachers were to be put to death (see Deuteronomy 13:5), and there were serious consequences for those who consulted them: "I will set my face against the person who turns to mediums and spiritists to prostitute himself by following them, and I will cut him off from his people" (Leviticus 20:6 NIV). Obviously we are not going to have an effective prayer time if God is cutting us off from Him and His people.

Second, *we are warned not to be deceived.* Deceived people are living in bondage to the lies they believe, and believing those lies seriously affects their walk with God. If Christians are paying attention to deceiving spirits, they are not paying attention to God. If they believe they need to defend themselves, they are not trusting Christ to be their defense. Certainly, no believer can instantly renew his or her mind, tear down mental strongholds, and overcome old defense mechanisms. But the process of renewing our minds won't even begin unless we are aware of our false beliefs and defenses—and God is willing to reveal them to us if we ask.

Third, *we need to forgive from our hearts as Christ has forgiven us.* We can't have an intimate relationship with God and hold bitterness in our hearts. Jesus said that our heavenly Father would turn us over to the torturers if we don't forgive (Matthew 18:34-35). It is hard to hear from God if our minds are tormented by thoughts about other people who have hurt us. So when we are trying to pray to God and our minds are plagued by thoughts of the injustices done to us by other people, we can know that God is allowing the mental torment so we will be driven to forgive others and seek forgiveness. In fact, some of these kinds of thoughts we struggle with are coming from Satan. Paul urges us to forgive, because we are not ignorant of Satan's schemes (2 Corinthians 2:11).*

When I encourage people to pray and ask God to reveal to their minds who they need to forgive, God does it. Sometimes people pray and then say there is nobody they need to forgive. When that happens, I just ask them to share with me the names that are coming to their minds—and out will come several names of people they need to forgive. Some may be hardening their hearts because they would rather seek revenge. Others are afraid to face their pain, so they live in denial or try to shove it down into the unconscious...but God is trying to surface the pain so they can let it go by forgiving.

Fourth, *we have to come to terms with our pride*. You cannot have a close relationship with God if He is opposed to you, but if you humbly ask, God will show you how prideful you have been. Notice how James connects pride with the world, flesh, and the devil:

> You ask and do not receive, because you ask with wrong motives, so that you may spend it on your own pleasures. You adulteresses, do you not know that friendship with the world is hostility toward God? Therefore whoever wishes to be a friend of the world makes himself an enemy of God. Or do you think that the Scripture speaks to no purpose: "He jealously desires the Spirit which He has made to dwell in us?" But He gives a greater grace. Therefore it says, "God is opposed to the proud, but gives grace to the humble" (4:3-7).

We can't pray by the Spirit and be prideful.

---

* The Greek word translated as "schemes" in this verse is *noema*. Elsewhere in 2 Corinthians it is translated as "thought" (10:5) or "minds" (4:4; 11:3).

Fifth, *we can't pray by the Spirit and be rebellious either.* Rebellion is as the sin of witchcraft and insubordination is as iniquity and idolatry (see 1 Samuel 15:23). God requires that all His children submit to governing authorities (Romans 13:1-7), parents (Ephesians 6:1-3), spouses (1 Peter 3:1-7; Ephesians 5:21-25), employers (1 Peter 2:18-23), church leaders (Hebrews 13:17), and God Himself (Daniel 9:5,9).

What happens in our courts of law when a rebellious prisoner approaches the bench disrespectfully? He is thrown out of court for contempt. The judge will not even hear from the accused—and neither will our heavenly Father hear from us in prayer if we approach Him disrespectfully and disobey His commands to submit to His established authority. If we ask Him, He will reveal our rebelliousness.

Sixth, *we can't expect God to hear our prayers if we are living in sin.* Rest assured He knows our sins and will bring conviction, so we aren't fooling anyone when we try to hide them. If they have never been acknowledged, these issues will plague our minds when we try to pray. That is what David tried to do, and he suffered for it. Finally, he turned to God—and later he recorded his experience in Psalm 32:1-6:

> How blessed is he whose transgression is forgiven, whose sin is covered! How blessed is the man to whom the LORD does not impute iniquity, and in whose spirit there is no deceit!
>
> When I kept silent about my sin, my body wasted away through my groaning all day long. For day and night Your hand was heavy upon me; my vitality was drained away as with the fever heat of summer...I acknowledged my sin to You, and my iniquity I did not hide; I said, "I will confess my transgressions to the LORD"; and You forgave the guilt of my sin...Therefore, let everyone who is godly pray to You in a time when You may be found;

surely in a flood of great waters they will not reach him.

Finally, *we cannot pray effectively if we continue in the sins of our ancestors.* Peter urged us,

> If you address as Father the One who impartially judges according to each one's work, conduct yourselves in fear during the time of your stay on earth; knowing that you were not redeemed with perishable things like silver or gold from *your futile way of life inherited from your forefathers*, but with precious blood, as of a lamb unblemished and spotless, the blood of Christ (1 Peter 1:17-19).

Sometimes we can be torn between our natural heritage and our spiritual heritage. Jesus is the sword that divides the family if our earthly parents and siblings are at odds with our heavenly Father. Our Savior said, "He who loves father or mother more than me is not worthy of Me; and he who loves son or daughter more than Me is not worthy of Me. And he who does not take his cross and follow after Me is not worthy of Me" (Matthew 10:37-38). Any attempt to hold a marriage or family together at the expense of our relationship with our heavenly Father is not in His plan. Compromising our faith to save a marriage doesn't work. The marriage won't be any good—and neither will our walk with God.

Under the Old Covenant, the Israelites confessed their sins and the sins of their fathers. This was necessary because people have a tendency to live according to how they have been taught. As Jesus noted, "A pupil is not above his teacher; but everyone, after he has been fully trained, will be like his teacher" (Luke 6:40). Nobody had more influence on us in our first five years than our parents, and unless we repent, we will live out the beliefs and values we have been taught...or caught from the environment of our homes. We are never guilty of our parents' sins, but because all parents have sinned, we have picked up some of their attitudes and actions that are not consistent with our Christianity.

Prayer That Is Effective

When Christians are encouraged to pray for God's guidance themselves, the results are dramatic. The Lord brings godly sorrow, and the Holy Spirit leads them into all truth, which is what sets them free. If they don't harden their hearts, they respond in repentance, which results in tremendous changes in their lives.[2]

James offers additional insight concerning effective prayer. "Confess your sins to one another, and pray for one another so that you may be healed. The effective prayer of a righteous man can accomplish much" (James 5:16). Notice the order of Scripture. The righteous person's prayer is effective *after* the person has confessed.

Suppose you are an elder or pastor of a church, and a member of your congregation who is ill calls for the elders to come and pray. So you dutifully respond to the request, and several elders join you in prayer, asking that God would intervene and heal the person. Then later you discover that the person is sexually promiscuous and is deeply bitter over a failed relationship. Do you expect God to answer those prayers? Actually, there is a very good chance that the sickness is the result of the person's sin. Most people are sick for psychosomatic reasons, and that is probably what the apostle James is primarily addressing in the passages from his epistle. In fact, psychosomatic illnesses are often related to sin (as with David's illness mentioned earlier).

Now suppose further that you have a son who is very rebellious. There is a lot of tension in your relationship. One day you tell him to mow the lawn, but he doesn't do it. Then later he comes and asks you for 20 dollars and the keys to the car—because he has a hot date. Would you give him the money and the keys? Would God? I don't think so. He would probably say, "Son, there are many unresolved issues between us. If you are willing to resolve them and mow the lawn like I told you, then we will talk about your date for this evening." I believe God allows His children to experience the natural consequences of their sins even though those sins are forgiven. I also believe He always stands ready to receive their prayers if they are willing to repent.

Amazing Answers

If people are willing to get right with God, then their prayers will accomplish much. I have seen incredible answers to prayer after people have gone through the Steps or repented in some other way. One woman shared that she had 200 doctor-certified allergies and that her children had more than a hundred. There were places they couldn't go, food they couldn't eat, and clothing they couldn't wear. All that disappeared when they prayed through those seven issues and found their freedom in Christ. This woman is now showing many others how they too can pray effectively.

An undergraduate student stopped by my office one day to ask some questions about her research project on Satanism. I answered a few of her questions, and then I told her, "I don't think you should be researching this subject." She asked me why not. I answered, "Because you're not experiencing your freedom in Christ." Surprised by my straightforwardness, she asked what I meant by that. I responded, "I'm sure your devotional life and prayer life are practically nonexistent. You probably have difficulty paying attention in your Bible classes, and I would suspect that you have a very low sense of worth. You probably entertain a lot of suicidal thoughts."

This student thought I had read her mind, which of course I hadn't. But I have had enough experience working with people so that I can discern their level of maturity and to what degree they are experiencing their freedom in Christ. I encouraged her to take my class on resolving personal and spiritual conflicts that coming summer. After the class, she wrote me this letter:

> What I've discovered this last week is a feeling of control, like my mind is my own. I haven't had my usual strung-out periods of thought and contemplation. My mind simply feels quieted.
>
> It really is a strange feeling. My emotions have been stable. I haven't felt depressed once this week. My will is mine. I feel like I have been able to choose to live my life abiding in Christ.
>
> Scripture seems different. I have a totally new perspective. I actually understand what it is saying. I feel left alone, but not in a bad way. I'm not lonely, just a single person. For the first time, I believe I actually understand what it means to be a Christian, who Christ is, and who I am in Him. I feel capable of helping people and capable of handling myself.
>
> I've been a co-dependent for years, but this last week I haven't had the slightest feeling or need for someone. I guess I'm describing what it is like to be at peace. I feel this quiet, soft joy in my heart. I have been more friendly and comfortable with strangers. It hasn't been a struggle to get through the day. And I have been participating actively in life and not merely passively, critically watching it. Thank you for lending me your hope. I believe I have my own now in Christ.

Because of her mental peace, this young woman is now able to hear from God in her daily life. Appropriating our identity and finding freedom in Christ through genuine repentance is what allows people to relate personally to God in prayer. Our ministry has the privilege of helping people all over the world find their identity and freedom in Christ. When they do, their prayer and devotional life come alive. If you hear His voice, don't harden your heart. Deal with the issues, and take every thought captive to the obedience of Christ.

QUESTIONS FOR THOUGHT AND DISCUSSION

1. Can we ask others to do our praying for us? Why or why not?

2. Why do you think most people ask others to do their praying for them?

3. Why does seeking false guidance hinder our prayers?

4. Why do deception, bitterness, pride, rebellion, and sin hinder our prayers?

5. How can iniquities passed on from one generation to the next hinder our prayers?

6. How does the Holy Spirit lead us into all truth, and why does that set us free?

7. What kind of results can we expect if God reveals our sins and we repent?

8. Can we expect God to answer the prayers of spiritual leaders on our behalf if we are living in sin?

9. Why are we not seeing more answers to prayer in our churches?

CHAPTER THREE

Progressing in Prayer

To be with God, there is no need to be continually in church. We may make an oratory of our heart wherein to retire from time to time to converse with Him in meekness, humility, and love. There is not in the world a kind of life more sweet and delightful than that of a continual conversation with God.

BROTHER LAWRENCE

IN MY 30-PLUS YEARS OF MINISTRY, I have seen three levels of prayer. Before we look at them, let me say that praise and thanksgiving should be a part of every level of prayer. To come before God with thanksgiving, as we touched on earlier, is no different than coming before our earthly parents with an attitude of gratitude. It is upsetting to parents when their children are always demanding, forever complaining, and never satisfied. How would you feel if you'd given as much as you could as a parent and your children still wanted more? On the other hand, how would you feel toward your children if they respectfully said, "Thank you for being who you are—I love you, and I know you're doing the best you can for me"?

Praising God is ascribing to Him His divine attributes. We should always be aware when we pray that God is our ever-present, all-powerful, all-knowing, and loving heavenly Father. Of course, God doesn't need us to tell Him who He is. He knows who He is. We are the ones who need to keep His divine attributes constantly in our minds. The knowledge of God's presence should be foremost in our thoughts. We ought to worship God by acknowledging His attributes and praying that He will grant us a consciousness of His presence.

Petition: The First Level of Prayer

Usually our petitions to God reflect people we know and things we care about. If it helps us to keep a list of daily prayer reminders, we should do so. It is certainly right to petition God. He invites us to let our requests be made known to Him (Philippians 4:6). James wrote, "You do not have because you do not ask" (4:2). There is no harm in asking, but then James cautions us about praying with wrong motives, which will hinder our prayer life (verse 3).

The Matter of Motives

If we come before God's presence with an attitude of gratitude and follow the example of the Lord's Prayer, our motives will be much purer. Jesus taught us,

> Pray, then, in this way: "Our Father who is in heaven, hallowed be Your name. Your kingdom come. Your will be done, on earth as it is in heaven. Give us this day our daily bread. And forgive us our debts, as we also have forgiven our debtors. And do not lead us into temptation, but deliver us from evil. [For Yours is the kingdom and the power and the glory forever. Amen]" (Matthew 6:9-13, brackets in original).

The first requirement is to have a right standing before our sovereign Lord. Very few citizens are granted an audience with earthly sovereigns. If you were granted that permission, you would have to approach respectfully. In some countries, not to do so could cost you your life. So what right do we have to bring our requests before the King of Kings? The writer of Hebrews says, "We have confidence to enter the holy place by the blood of Jesus" (Hebrews 10:19). When we pray in the name of Jesus, we do so with the understanding that we have no right to approach the throne of God except on the basis of the efficacious work of Jesus. Because of Jesus, we are children of God by faith and joint heirs with His Son. This position in Christ, which every believer has, is what affords us access to our heavenly Father. That is why we pray in the name of Jesus.

Jesus is our advocate with our heavenly Father right now (1 John 2:1). Even if we do sin and the devil accuses us (see Zechariah 3:1-5), Jesus is standing at the right hand of God and saying, "Look at the wounds in My hands and My feet. I died for that person's sins, and I was resurrected so they would have eternal life." Being joint heirs with Jesus gives us access to the throne of God, and we have the right to be there since we are God's children.

We affirm our reverence for God when we pray "Hallowed be Your name"—"May Your name be honored as holy." Worship is always an integral part of Spirit-directed prayer because worshiping God is ascribing to Him the divine attributes that He alone possesses. Knowing the nature of God and His ways shapes our prayers. For instance, we don't have to ask the Lord to "be with the missionaries," because He is omnipresent and therefore always is with the missionaries. If we know the true nature of God, we won't ask Him to protect us from our indiscretions by covering up our sin or lying for us, because He is light and in Him there is no darkness at all, and He cannot lie. True worship is done in Spirit and in truth—and so are effective prayers.

Motives Shaped by God's Motives

Second, we must approach God with requests that are consistent with His kingdom plans and His will. God is not going to help us establish our own kingdom and enable us to do whatever we will. We don't make plans and ask God to bless them, we ask God for His plans and then commit ourselves to follow them. Certainly, God will be there in a crisis—but we shouldn't think of prayer as a fourth-down punting situation. Effective prayer is a first-down huddle during which we are receiving our next play from the coach. "This is the confidence which we have before Him, that, if we ask anything according to His will, He hears us" (1 John 5:14).

When I was a pastor, a member of our church was dying with cancer. His wife wouldn't let me pray for her husband if I ended the prayer by saying, "If it be according to your will." She thought that was a cop-out. Rather, I was supposed to *demand* that God heal her husband. This saddened me because there was nothing I wanted more for my friend than God's will, and there is nothing I want more for myself. Do you believe that the will of God is good, acceptable, and perfect for you (Romans 12:2)? If you worship God in Spirit and truth, you will desire nothing other than the will of God.

If that wasn't enough deception to choke off the Spirit of God, four independent witnesses all said that my friend was going to be healed, and the news of this "revelation" spread throughout the church. "Isn't that great, Pastor? The Lord told four people he's going to be healed!" Three weeks later my friend died, so I guess that makes God a liar. Wrong! "It is impossible for God to lie" (Hebrews 6:18). Those four witnesses weren't hearing from God—they were paying attention to deceiving spirits whose purpose was to discredit God.

Motives Governed by Our Needs, Not Our Wants

The phrase from the Lord's prayer, "Give us this day our daily bread," implies that we should ask God for our needs, and not our wants. The psalmist wrote, "Delight yourself in the LORD; and He will give you the desires of your heart" (Psalm 37:4). He won't give us the desires of our flesh, but if we delight in Him, our desires will change and be consistent with what He deems best for us. The truth is, we don't always know what is best for us. That is why we must trust God when He says "no" to some of our requests, and "yes" or "later" when they are right for us.

Catherine Marshall, author of the well-known novel *Christy*, was the wife of Peter Marshall, the famous pastor whose life was depicted in the movie *A Man Called Peter*. During the course of their pastoral ministry, Catherine fell sick and was bedridden for a year. Nobody could really explain her illness, and nobody's prayers seemed to make any difference. They tried every possible remedy, but to no avail. Finally, Catherine prayed a prayer of relinquishment. I don't know her exact words, but the essence of her prayer was, "Lord, I give up trying to fix myself and trying to persuade You to heal me or give me some explanation as to why I am sick. I accept this illness as Your will, and I relinquish my right to determine what is best for me. You have the right to do with my life whatever You choose. If You want me to be sick for some purpose I don't know, then I accept that as Your will for my life, since I belong to You. Amen." Within four days, she was out of bed, and she fully recovered.

Petitioning God for our "daily bread" affirms our dependency upon Him. As a further example, a prayer of thanksgiving before a meal is a means of acknowledging that all good things come from God. If our daily needs are met, it is easier to stand up against temptations, which are attempts by the enemy to get us to live our lives independently of God.

Finally, in order to purify our motives in approaching God with our petitions, we should forgive others as we expect Him to forgive us. In the previous chapter I discussed the futility of praying to God while harboring bitterness in our hearts. God will enable us to forgive, and He will answer our prayer when we ask Him who we need to forgive. Anything He asks us to do, He will enable us to do. I have been taught to believe that "the will of God will never take you where the grace of God cannot keep you."

Personal, Two-Way Prayer: The Second Level

If prayer consisted only of petitions, many of us would not linger very long in prayer. If we don't see any answers to our petitions, we are tempted to think that we can accomplish more if we start "doing something" for the Lord. If that is the case, then our service for God will be the greatest enemy of our devotion to Him. We can get tired of petitioning God when the communication seems to be one-way. Some are motivated by guilt to continue petitioning God even though their hearts aren't in it. In sum, when our devotional times consist of petitions only, this leads to stagnant growth, fruitless living, and disappointment with God.

The second level of prayer is personal and two-way. You have entered into a new dimension of spirituality when you are comfortable in His presence and don't feel obligated to talk. It's like a good marriage. A mature couple can ride together in the same car for hours, enjoying each other's company without having to say a word. However, if you are alone with a stranger, silence is awkward.

Realizing that it was okay to be silent in God's presence changed my prayer life. I could actually rest in His presence. Those who learn to "practice His presence" have learned to "pray without ceasing" (1 Thessalonians 5:17). When I discovered this as a pastor, I started to commune with God as I rode my bicycle to church, when I called on people, spoke in churches, and counseled others. I now practice this communion when I write books. Stories, illustrations, scriptural passages, and new insights come to me in a way I can't explain apart from God, and so the end product of every book I have written has been different than what I thought it was going to be when I started. God is always present, but now I am more aware of His presence. Personal prayer makes a relationship with God a 24-hour-a-day experience. Setting aside special time for prayer and devotions is still important, but when I leave my quiet times, I leave with God—and prayer doesn't stop!

True Intercession: The Third Level of Prayer

When prayer becomes personal between God and His child, then true intercession is possible. True intercessors hear from God. They know how to pray and what to pray for because the Holy Spirit is interceding for them in ways that can't be explained.

In my observation, there are very few true intercessory prayer warriors. They are all mature saints, and the most effective ones are women, though both men and women can be equally effective. These intercessors pray privately in their homes, often at night. When God wakes them up, they know who and what to pray for, and they stay in prayer until God releases them. If you make their ministry known publicly and put them in a spotlight, you will destroy their effectiveness. If you are in church leadership, find out who the prayer warriors are in your congregation. Every church has at least one or two of them. Share your schedule and family needs with them. When these people pray, things happen, because their prayers originate in heaven.

Choosing Truth, Dispelling Darkness

The three levels of prayer may correlate with the three levels of growth depicted in 1 John 2:12-14. John describes those who have their sins forgiven as "little children." They have overcome the penalty of their sins by the grace of God. At the highest level, according to John, are old people in the faith who have a deep reverential knowledge of God. Then notice how

John describes young people in the faith: "I write to you, young men, because you are strong, and the word of God lives in you, and you have overcome the evil one" (verse 14 NIV). Those who have reached the second level have learned how to overcome the power of sin.

Learning to overcome the evil one is essential for mental peace and effective prayer. It is impossible to be led by the Holy Spirit if you are paying attention to an evil spirit. Tempting, accusing, and deceiving thoughts can be very distracting. If you are attempting to deal with deceiving thoughts by trying to rebuke them, you'll be like the person treading water in the middle of the ocean while trying to keep 12 corks submerged with a little hammer! You will survive for a while, but you will make no progress—and the devil will have all your attention. Rather, we should ignore the corks and swim to shore! We shouldn't pay attention to deceiving spirits. We are not called to dispel the darkness—we are called to turn on the light. The key is to get rid of the deceptive thoughts and that is what you will have an opportunity to do in chapter 7.

Scripture doesn't tell us not to think bad thoughts—it instructs us to choose the truth. The darkness is dispelled when we turn on the light. If you are plagued by tempting thoughts, bring the basis for the temptation before God and seek to resolve any personal and spiritual conflicts that are keeping you from having an intimate relationship with Him. The schemes of the devil are not our focus—he is only taking advantage of the fact that our intimacy with God has been broken through our own sin and rebellion. Satan knows that if he can keep our minds distracted, we won't have much of a prayer life with God, and personal prayer is essential for us to receive God's guidance. If we are going to walk with God, we must have the peace of God that will "guard our hearts and minds in Christ Jesus" (Philippians 4:7).

Spiritual Protection

The armor of God provides all the spiritual protection we need. When we put on the armor of God (see Ephesians 6:10-20), we are putting on the Lord Jesus Christ (see Romans 13:12-14). There is no physical place that can serve as a spiritual sanctuary, our only sanctuary is our position in Christ. We stand against Satan's deception by girding our loins with truth (Ephesians 6:14). We stand against Satan's accusations by putting on the breastplate of righteousness (verse 14). That piece of the armor is not *our* righteousness, it is the righteousness of *Christ*. Those who put on the Lord Jesus Christ become instruments of peace because they are united with the Prince of Peace. Taking up the shield of faith is what protects us from Satan's flaming arrows (verse 16). When we put on the helmet of salvation, we are taking our rightful place in Christ. Armed with His power and authority, we use the sword of the Spirit, which is the Word of God. The truth of God's Word is what keeps the father of lies at bay.

We cannot passively take our place in Christ. We have to actively choose to believe who we are and all that Christ has done for us. What is often overlooked in regard to the armor of God is our responsibility. *"Take up* the full armor of God, so that you will be able to resist in the evil day, and having done everything, to stand firm. *Stand firm* therefore..." (Ephesians 6:13-14). God has provided all the protection we need, but it will be ineffective if we don't assume our responsibility to stand firm in our faith.

Prayer—The Essential Weapon

Many Christians think that the list of the pieces of armor ends with the sword, but it doesn't. Prayer is the essential weapon in spiritual warfare, as Paul explains in verses 18-20 of Ephesians 6:

> With all prayer and petition *pray at all times in the Spirit*, and with this in view, be on the alert with all perseverance and petition for all the saints, and pray on my behalf, that utterance may be given to me in the opening of my mouth, to make known with boldness the mystery of the gospel, for which I am an ambassador in chains; that in proclaiming it I may speak boldly, as I ought to speak.

Holy Spirit–directed prayer affects the spiritual realm more than the physical realm. The devil blinds the minds of the unbelieving (2 Corinthians 4:4) and deceives the whole world (Revelation 12:9). Consequently, the whole world lies in the power of the evil one (1 John 5:19). That is why Christians must break through to level two and three to be effective prayer warriors. During this church age God has committed Himself to work through Christians who have overcome the evil one and are filled with His Holy Spirit. These Spirit-directed believers do kingdom work, and their prayers thwart the activities of Satan. This is where intercessory prayer is most effective, and those who are led to pray in this way are fulfilling God's eternal purpose, as Paul explains in Ephesians 3:8-12:

> To me, the very least of all saints, this grace was given, to preach to the Gentiles the unfathomable riches of Christ, and to bring to light what is the administration of the mystery [something not previously revealed] which for ages has been hidden in God who created all things; so that the manifold wisdom of God might now be made known through the church to the rulers and authorities in the heavenly places [the spiritual realm]. This was in accordance with the eternal purpose which He carried out in Christ Jesus our Lord, in whom we have boldness and confident access through faith in Him.

QUESTIONS FOR THOUGHT
AND DISCUSSION

1. Describe your personal experience of the three levels of prayer identified in this chapter: petition, personal, intercession.

2. Explain how our motives for praying are purified by following the example of the Lord's prayer.

3. When should we pray a prayer of relinquishment, and when should we persevere in prayer?

4. How are communion with God, personal prayer, and praying without ceasing intertwined?

5. How does John characterize little children, young men, and old men of the faith? How can we relate this to prayer?

6. What does prayer have to do with spiritual warfare?

7. Is putting on the armor of God a prerequisite for praying in the Spirit? Why or why not?

8. Which realm is most affected by prayer, the physical or the spiritual? Why?

9. How should this affect your personal prayer life?

CHAPTER FOUR

Interceding in Prayer

*The first thing I do, after having asked in a few words
the Lord's blessing upon His precious Word,
is to begin to meditate on the Word of God, searching
as it were into every verse to get blessing out of
it...for the sake of obtaining food for my soul. The
result I have found to be almost invariably this, that
after a few minutes my soul has been led to
confession, or to thanksgiving, or to intercession, or
to supplication; so that, though I did not, as it were,
give myself to prayer but to meditation, it had turned
almost immediately more or less into prayer.*

GEORGE MUELLER

On ONE OF MY TRIPS TO SOUTH AMERICA, I talked with two
pastors who were planning to resign from their churches and
run for public office. They thought they could accomplish more
if they had political positions of influence and power. I respectfully disagreed with them. These pastors were forsaking their
calling and the spiritual authority they had over the spiritual
kingdom of darkness, which manipulates earthly rulers. Believers have the potential of accomplishing more by virtue of
their position in Christ than they can by obtaining any earthly

position. Think how Christ has impacted this world without having held any ecclesiastical or political office. He showed us what a child of God could accomplish if rightly related to the Father.

Our Attitude in Praying for Those in Authority over Us

Concerning earthly rulers, Paul instructed us to pray this way:

> First of all, then, I urge that entreaties and prayers, petitions and thanksgiving, be made on behalf of all men, for kings and all who are in authority, so that we may lead a tranquil and quiet life in all godliness and dignity. This is good and acceptable in the sight of God our Savior, who desires all men to be saved and to come to the knowledge of the truth. For there is one God, and one mediator also between God and men, the man Christ Jesus (1 Timothy 2:1-5).

It is counterproductive for the church to be at odds with civil government. God has given the church spiritual authority, and the government civil authority (see Romans 13:1-8). The church is not the ruler of the state, but we are the conscience of the state—and we have authority over the god of this world. Non-Christian leaders are walking "according to the course of this world, according to the prince of the power of the air [Satan], of the spirit that is now working in the sons of disobedience" (Ephesians 2:2). Peter gave instruction on how a liberated Christian should respond to them:

> Submit yourselves for the Lord's sake to every human institution, whether to a king as the one in authority, or to governors sent by him for the pun-

ishment of evildoers and the praise of those who do right. For such is the will of God that by doing right you may silence the ignorance of foolish men. Act as free men, and do not use your freedom as a covering for evil, but use it as bondslaves of God. Honor all people, love the brotherhood, fear God, honor the king (1 Peter 2:13-17).

We cannot be right with God and rebel against His established authority. It must grieve God to hear Christian leaders and followers speaking negatively against civil government and its leadership. I am fully aware that every country in the world has some despicable leaders, but it is their position that we respect, not their person. Christian leadership should set an example by being submissive to civic leaders and praying for those in authority over them. Politicians don't respect the church when we point our fingers at them, because they know we have our own problems. How hypocritical is that? Jesus warned us about seeing the speck in another's eye while ignoring the plank in our own eyes (Matthew 7:1-5). Besides, judgment begins in the household of God. Many politicians don't see the church as an ally. In fact many see the church as their arch enemy. Shame on us.

Two Ways to Pray

Let me suggest two ways we can pray for those in authority over us. First, we should pray that God will enable them to be instruments of justice in our land, and especially, we should pray for any specific needs they may have. We won't know about these needs unless we ask. I encourage representatives from local ministries to make appointments with local civic leaders and ask them how they as a Christian community can pray for them.

One such delegation approached a feminist politician, who was more than ready for them. With her guard fully up, she greeted them by saying, "I just want you to know that I am prochoice and a feminist." They responded by saying, "Ma'am, that is your choice, but that is not why we are here. You are our elected representative, and we came to ask how we could pray for you so that your term in office would be a success." That caught her totally by surprise and left her speechless. Finally, she responded with some personal needs she had and thanked them for coming. Within a year her voting record began to change.

Such an approach is following the example of the Lord's prayer. These pastors were approaching an authority figure with the intent of helping her fulfill her responsibilities. Politicians have a huge responsibility, and many of them realize their task is impossible without the support of others. So they are not inclined to refuse prayer.

The same holds for petitioning your superiors at work. They don't like an employee who makes their job harder. So if you approach your bosses with the desire to help them be more successful, they are probably going to listen to what you have to say. What do you think would happen if you said to your bosses, "I know you have a big job and a lot of responsibility—how can my family and I pray for you?" Your petitions, requests, and suggestions are more likely to be considered if they help the one you are petitioning be more successful. Wouldn't it profit you more if the leadership over you were more successful in carrying out their responsibilities? On the other hand, your job and career could be in jeopardy if they aren't successful. An unwillingness to support them, in the hope that they will fail so you can get their position, is not considering the other person more important than yourself (see Philippians 2:1-5)—and it will likely cause others to be disloyal to you because of your example.

I believe the church community should also pray for civil servants who protect us from criminals and from fires and other disasters. A group of pastors in one city approached their chief of police, who was anything but a Christian, and said, "We really appreciate all that our police department is doing for us, and we are concerned for their safety. Would it be possible to get a list of all our policemen and distribute each of their names to churches in their own districts so we as a Christian community can pray for their protection and safety?" The police chief was so astonished by their request that he called in his assistant and said, "Give them whatever they want." The same holds true for our firemen and teachers in public schools. We will lead a more tranquil and quiet life in all godliness and dignity if we pray this way.

Second, we should pray for our leaders' salvation. People in authority need the Lord like everyone else does. Praying for their needs may give us the opportunity to love them into the arms of the Lord. After all, we can't *preach* the good news and *be* the bad news. If our leaders sense we really care for them, they are going to be far more responsive to what we say. Remember, God "desires all men to be saved and to come to the knowledge of the truth" (1 Timothy 2:4).

Praying for a Messenger to the Lost

In my first pastorate, I briefly discipled a young man fresh out of college. His mother attended our church, but his father, who was divorced from his mother, wasn't a believer. This young man married and went on the mission field. For the next 25 years he prayed for his father's salvation, but to no avail. Finally he gave up in frustration and essentially said to God, "For 25 years I have prayed for my father and nothing has happened. I see no need to pray any longer because it doesn't seem to be doing any good." Well, the Lord had done all that He needed to do—all that remained was for this missionary to pray the way Scripture instructed him to pray.

How then should we pray—or not pray—for the lost? First, we don't have to pray that Jesus would convict unbelievers of their sins. You can claim that as a promise because Jesus said that the Holy Spirit "will convict the world concerning sin and righteousness and judgment" (John 16:8). Second, however, we should pray that God send the unbeliever someone who will be a good witness. Jesus said to His disciples, "The harvest is plentiful, but the workers are few. Therefore beseech the Lord of the harvest to send out workers into His harvest" (Matthew 9:37-38). In this vein, Paul wrote in Romans 10:13-15,

> "Whoever will call upon the name of the Lord will be saved." How then will they call on Him in whom they have not believed? How will they believe in Him whom they have not heard? And how will they hear without a preacher? How will they preach unless they are sent? Just as it is written, "How beautiful are the feet of those who bring good news of good things!"

The missionary I mentioned started to pray that God would send his father a preacher or a messenger. Six weeks later he received a letter from his father that essentially read, "Son, I thought you would like to know that somebody in my apartment invited me to a Bible study a few weeks back, and I have decided to become a Christian."

Jesus declared that the fields are white for harvest (John 4:35), and we should be praying for workers and humbly asking God to send them out. Let me illustrate how this works. A church was giving the chairman of our board a banquet celebrating his 25 years of pastoral leadership, and I was invited to be the speaker. Then I spoke at the church worship services the next morning, and after that we had lunch together. He and his wife expressed their disappointment that one of their sons hadn't come to the services. I shared with them the story of my missionary friend, and I suggested that we pray and ask God to send their son a messenger.

Tuesday morning I received a telephone call. "You aren't going to believe it, but my son called me last night." A few hours after the parents and I had prayed, their son was invited to attend a Bible study on Monday evening. At the Bible study, they found out that his father was a pastor and told him they needed someone to lead them. In accord with their request, this young man called later that Monday evening and asked his father if he would lead the Bible study. He did this for the next year. Five years later, I was asked to speak again, this time at the pastor's thirtieth anniversary—and the once wayward son emceed the program.

I was teaching a Doctor of Ministry class at Trinity Evangelical Divinity School. On the first morning I taught (a Monday), an older pastor from another class greeted me and wanted to discuss how to make better use of our material in his church. Later that day he had an urgent prayer request. His son-in-law was an officer in the air force who was stationed in Saudi Arabia. He was so depressed that he was suicidal. I told him the above about prayer, and I suggested we ask the Lord to send his son-in-law a messenger, someone who could help him.

Friday morning this pastor was waiting to tell me some good news. "You won't believe this [no, I *would*] but some time after we prayed a senior officer who was a Christian contacted my son-in-law. Last night my son-in-law called and said everything is okay." This man had found the help he needed—and God had sent it to him.

Praying for Life for the Lost

There is a second thing we should pray for concerning the lost. The apostle John wrote in 1 John 5:12-17,

> He who has the Son has the life; he who does not have the Son of God does not have the life (verse 12).
>
> These things I have written to you who believe in the name of the Son of God, so that you may know that you have eternal life (verse 13). This is the confidence which we have before Him, that, if we ask anything according to His will, He hears us (verse 14). And if we know that He hears us in whatever we

ask, we know that we have the requests which we have asked from Him (verse 15).

If anyone sees his brother committing a sin not leading to death, he shall ask and God will for him give life to those who commit sin not leading to death. There is a sin leading to death; I do not say that he should make request for this (verse 16). All unrighteousness is sin, and there is a sin not leading to death (verse 17).

I have included the larger context of verse 16 because it is important to see that John is talking about *spiritual* life and death (*zoe* in the Greek), not *physical* life and death. What Adam and Eve lost in the fall was spiritual life (*zoe*). Consequently, we are all born dead (that is, physically alive but spiritually dead) in our trespasses and sins (Ephesians 2:1), and Jesus came to give us life (John 10:10).

John is telling the reader that God will answer prayer if it is according to His will. Then he gives a specific illustration of intercessory prayer for those who have not committed a sin leading to death. By writing "he shall ask," John is not giving a command—he is referring to the inevitable and spontaneous prayers of believers who are so led.

To quickly explain one of John's terms, the "sin leading to death" is similar to the blasphemy of the Holy Spirit. It is the unique work of the Holy Spirit to draw us to Christ and to make the finished work of Christ known. If we reject that witness, as the Pharisees did, then we never come to the Christ who died for our sins. Essentially this is the sin of unbelief, and no Christian can commit this sin, because all Christians are already alive and forgiven in Christ. However, the Pharaoh of Egypt hardened his own heart three times in spite of the miracles that Moses performed, as we see in the first part of Exodus. From that time on, God hardened his heart. That is an example of the sin leading to death. (But since we really don't know the condition of another person's heart, but God does, we should pray for whoever God lays on our hearts.)

We Are Called to Participate

John's words in this important passage are often viewed as not applying to our praying for the lost because people assume that the word "brother" (verse 16) in Scripture always refers to a born-again believer. However, the term *brother* can be used in the broader sense of "neighbor" or of someone in attendance at Christian meetings. This is implied in the teachings of Jesus (see Matthew 5:22-24; 7:3-5) and of James (5:19-20). *Brother* can refer to the affection in which the person is regarded, and not necessarily to their standing or character.

The critical point John is making in regard to such a "brother," as John Stott points out, is that "he is given life in answer to prayer. This means that, although his sin is 'not unto death,' he is in fact dead and needs to be given life."[3]

If we take this passage from 1 John literally (and we should), then we have to conclude that God has chosen the prayers of His children to be part of the salvation process ("he shall ask and God will...give life"). That does not mean we can decide for ourselves who we want to be saved and their salvation is assured simply because we choose to pray. There are other players in the process, namely God and the faith-choice of the sinner. Jesus declared, "No one can come to Me unless the Father who sent Me draws him; and I will raise him up on the last day" (John 6:44). I believe that God is sovereign over the salvation process—but in His sovereignty, He has chosen to work through His church. He commissioned us to go into the world, called us to be witnesses, and told us to pray in such a way that we would hear from heaven.

After explaining to groups how to pray in the Spirit, I use this passage in 1 John as an example. On behalf of the congregation, I invite the Holy Spirit to lay on their hearts the people He wants them to pray for. Then I invite them to share out loud the names that are coming to their minds. Within a matter of seconds, names are being spoken all over the auditorium. After a minute or two, the room starts to grow silent—and then a second round of names are expressed, and some people begin to cry. There is a good chance that the first round of names includes people the audience is concerned about (as they should be)…and that the second round of names is coming from God.

When we humbly pray that God would give unbelievers life and ask Him to send a messenger, we shouldn't be surprised to find out later that we are the messengers God had in mind. In fact, those who have a personal prayer life with God have probably been the messengers whom God has sent in response to other people's prayers.

Praying Against the Blinding of the Lost

There is a third part that we play in praying for the lost. In 2 Corinthians 4:3-4, Paul wrote,

> If our gospel is veiled, it is veiled to those who are perishing, in whose case the god of this world has blinded the minds of the unbelieving so that they might not see the light of the gospel of the glory of Christ, who is the image of God.

How are we going to reach the lost for Christ if Satan has blinded their minds? It should be obvious that this requires spiritual warfare in prayer. Theodore Epp gave an insightful answer in his little book *Praying with Authority:*

> It is true that Satan's power has been broken (Heb. 2:14,15; Col. 2:15), but we must recognize that he will not turn loose of anything he thinks he can keep, until we exercise the authority delegated to us by the Lord Jesus Christ. Prayer is not our trying to persuade God to join us in service for Him. It is our

joining Him in His service. True prayer on the part of the Christian is laying hold by faith of property that Satan has his hands on but which rightfully belongs to God—and then holding on until Satan turns loose. The Evil One will hold on to these souls until we take our place, demanding their release on the basis of the authority we have in Christ.[4]

Praying for the Rebellious Believer

The Old Testament book of Hosea is about God's love for Israel in spite of her unfaithfulness. This is vividly depicted by Hosea's marriage to his unfaithful wife Gomer. Hosea remained faithful to Gomer and wrote this, which also reflects God's way of dealing with His rebellious people:

> I will hedge up her way with thorns, and I will build a wall against her so that she cannot find her paths. She will pursue her lovers, but she will not overtake them; and she will seek them, but will not find them. Then she will say, "I will go back to my first husband, for it was better for me then than now" (2:6-7).

In modern parlance, Hosea is saying, "I am not going to be an enabler for her. I am going to let her experience the natural consequences of her behavior. As this happens, others will lose interest in her, and she will return home to me because she will come to understand that this is better for her." This reasoning is very similar to that of the father who let his prodigal son experience the natural consequences of his sin. Going home was the only option when he finally came to his senses.

This should also set a pattern for how we pray for the rebellious. "Lord, 'hedge up their way with thorns.'" We pray this way in the hope that God will cause all harmful influences to leave her, or him. The hedge of thorns will keep them away. I also recommend that you pray, "Lord, do what You have to do in order for them to come to their senses, but spare their lives." Whether the rebel is one of your children or your spouse, your prayers are functioning like a spiritual intervention. If they aren't believers, then you should pray that God would send them a messenger and give them life, and you should take authority over the blinding tactics of Satan.

Nobody likes to see loved ones suffer, but suffering is one means God uses to get our attention. If you start to pray for your loved ones to experience sin's consequences, you should also start preparing for them to come home by making this an easy decision. Hosea wrote, "I will allure her, bring her into the wilderness [a neutral place] and speak kindly to her. Then I will give her her vineyards from there, and the valley of Achor as a door of hope. And she will sing there as in the days of her youth" (2:14-15). Many people who have ruined their lives need to be given new hope and new opportunity.

I shared this message with my congregation a number of years back, and a dear mother came to see me two weeks later. She said, "I have been praying for my wayward daughter as you suggested, but it didn't work. Everything got worse for her. She lost her job, and her roommate moved out, leaving her with payments she can't afford." God did answer this mother's prayers, but she couldn't see it at first because she didn't want her daughter to suffer. I would—if that were what it took to bring her home.

Paul even instructs us to deliver such a wayward person "to Satan for the destruction of his flesh, so that his spirit may be saved in the day of the Lord Jesus" (1 Corinthians 5:5). Let the rebellious experience the natural consequences of living in this fallen world, if that is what it takes to save their souls. I admit that it is not easy to watch our children struggle when we want so much for them...but what choice do we have? Do we want them to try to be happy apart from God for a few years on this planet—or do we want them to suffer the loss of all things so that they may gain Christ (Philippians 3:7-8)?

God Answers

When Satan questioned God about the devotion His people had toward Him, God pointed to Job as the most righteous man on the earth (Satan's kingdom). "Then Satan answered the LORD, 'Does Job fear God for nothing? Have you not made a hedge about him and his house and all that he has, on every side?'" (Job 1:9-10). God can and does put hedges of protection around His children. I often pray that God would put a hedge of protection around me, my family, my possessions, and my ministry. God can also remove that protection if it serves a greater purpose, as was the case with Job. Should God do that for the purpose of testing us, remember that He will make everything right in the end, as He did for Job. (I share my own experience with this in chapter 6.)

Intercessory prayer is always consistent with Scripture, and it is effective when our prayers originate in heaven. God's children filled with His Spirit are praying, God is answering, and the kingdom of God is expanding. The letters written to the seven churches in Revelation 2–3 all end with the same exhortation: "He who has an ear, let him hear what the Spirit says to the churches" (2:7). Are we listening?

QUESTIONS FOR THOUGHT
AND DISCUSSION

1. What attitude should we have toward politicians in author-
    ity over us?

2. How could you personally pray for civil servants?

3. How should you pray for the lost?

4. Have you ever been a messenger sent by God?

5. Have you ever been awakened by God to pray for others?

6. How should you pray for a rebellious child or friend?

7. What does the hedge of thorns do?

CHAPTER FIVE

Living by the Spirit

*One only asks God to do through another what
he is willing for the Lord to do through him. That is
the law of intercession on every level of life. Only
so far as we have been tested and proved willing to do
a thing ourselves can we intercede for others. Christ
is an Intercessor, because he took the place of each
one prayed for. We are never called to intercede
for sin—that has been done once and for all;
but we are often called to intercede for sinners and
their needs, and the Holy Spirit can never "bind the
strong man" through us on a higher level than that
in which he has first had victory in us.*

REES HOWELLS

A YOUNG PILOT HAD JUST PASSED THE POINT of no return when
the weather changed for the worse. Visibility dropped to a
matter of feet as fog descended. Putting total trust in the cockpit
instruments was a new experience for him, for the ink was still wet
on the certificate verifying that he was qualified for instrument
flying.

The landing worried him the most. His destination was a
crowded metropolitan airport that he wasn't familiar with. In a

few minutes he would be in radio contact with the tower. Until then, he was alone with his thoughts. Flying with no visibility, he became aware of how easy it would be to panic. He twice reached for the radio to broadcast "Mayday!" but instead he forced himself to go over and over the words of his instructor. His flight instructor had required him to practically memorize the rulebook. He didn't care for this at the time, but now he was thankful.

Finally he heard the voice of the air-traffic controller. Trying not to sound apprehensive, the young pilot asked for landing instructions. "I'm going to put you in a holding pattern," the controller responded. *Great!* thought the pilot. He knew that his safe landing was in the hands of this person. Again he had to draw upon his previous flight instruction and trust the voice of an air-traffic controller he couldn't see. The words of an old hymn, "Trust and obey, for there's no other way," took on new meaning. Aware that this was no time for pride, he informed the controller, "This is not a seasoned pro up here. I would appreciate any help you could give me." "You got it!" he heard back.

For the next 45 minutes, the controller gently guided the pilot through the blinding fog. As course and altitude corrections came periodically, the young pilot realized the controller was guiding him around obstacles and away from potential collisions. With the words of the instruction book in his mind, and with the gentle voice of the controller, he landed safely.

The Holy Spirit guides us through the maze of life much like that air-traffic controller. The controller assumed that the young pilot understood the instructions in the flight manual, and his guidance was based on that. Such is the case with the Holy Spirit—He can guide us only if we have the knowledge of God's Word established in our minds. This combination of God's Word and the Holy Spirit's guidance is the basis for walking by the Spirit, which we need to do if we are going to pray by the Spirit. Therefore, in this chapter we'll take a thorough look at how believers walk by the Spirit and are led by the Spirit.

The Urgent Need

Early in church history, the Jerusalem council convened to discuss two critical issues that were threatening the body of believers (see Acts 15). One issue was circumcision, and the other was socializing with the use of foods that weren't kosher. They were debating the boundaries of legalism and license. That tension still exists today.

It is important to note how the early Christians finally came to an agreement. First, they searched the Scriptures: "With this the words of the prophets agree, just as it is written" (Acts 15:15). After consulting the Scriptures, they drafted a letter that was sent with Paul, two phrases of which read, "having become of one mind" and "for it seemed good to the Holy Spirit and to us" (verses 25,28). Their search for guidance through their crisis was balanced—they consulted the Scriptures and came to the mind of Christ by the aid of the Holy Spirit.

We desperately need God's guidance through the moral demise of our country. In too many cases our only response to immorality is to emphasize the moral standards of the law. We see divorce, so we preach against divorce. We see drunkenness, so we preach against the excessive use of alcohol. We see drugs, so we preach against drugs. How is it working? Proclaiming the law has never worked and it never will! Tolerating sin doesn't work either. Neither legalism nor license can stem the tide of moral decay. What we need, the answer for overcoming sin, is taught in Galatians 5:16-18:

> I say, walk by the Spirit, and you will not carry out the desires of the flesh. For the flesh sets its desire against the Spirit, and the Spirit against the flesh; for these are in opposition to one another, so that

you may not do the things that you please. But if
you are led by the Spirit, you are not under the Law.

The flight instruction manual is the authority according to
which we fly. But who would deny that the plane is empowered
by something other than the pilot, or question the need for an air-
traffic controller? We need the guidance of the Holy Spirit, but
how do we walk or live by the Spirit? If I answered these questions
with a three-step formula, I'd be putting you back under the law.
To walk by the Spirit is not a legal issue—it's a personal issue. Air-
traffic controllers are living people, not prerecorded voices
based on predictable weather conditions. The Holy Spirit is not
an "it"—the Holy Spirit is a *He*.

The above passage from Galatians explains more what
walking by the Spirit is not, rather than what it is. But knowing
that is helpful, because it provides boundaries within which we
live. So let's consider what walking by the Spirit is not.

Walking by the Spirit Is Not License

We first learn from the above passage that walking by the
Spirit is not license. *License* is an excessive or undisciplined
lifestyle constituting the abuse of a privilege. To be *licentious*
means that a person lacks moral discipline and has no regard for
accepted rules and regulations. If we walk by the Spirit we won't
carry out the desires of the flesh, and we won't do whatever we
please.

When I was born, I was completely dependent upon my
mother and father for human survival. If they hadn't fed me,
changed my diapers, and taken care of me, I would have died. Like
most children, I started to exert my independence at about the
age of two. (Can't you just hear a little child saying, "I can do it,"
"I want to do it myself"?) So my parents, like all good parents, set
boundaries. It is not safe or good training to let children have
their own way.

Now that we are children of God, the presence of the Holy Spirit brings us sorrow when we try to please the flesh. If there were no moral restraints and no boundaries to govern our behavior, we would all slide into moral decadence. Imagine the air-traffic controller saying to the pilot, "You have my permission to land any time and any place you want." That pilot would probably crash and burn!

Paul wrote, "You were called to freedom, brethren; only do not turn your freedom into an opportunity for the flesh, but through love serve one another" (Galatians 5:13). God wants us to be free, but freedom is not license. We are free by the grace of God to live a responsible life.

In the first half of the twentieth century, rigid fundamentalism left many churches frozen in legalism. In the '60s this legalism began to thaw through the Jesus movement. The pendulum swung from an emphasis on the justice of God to an emphasis on the mercy of God, and many in the American culture went from legalism to license. Some reasoned, "Since I am under the grace of God, I can do whatever I want—and there is no way a God of love would send me to hell." Why not have free sex and free drugs? Because exercising license always comes with a price. The number of people who have died or whose lives have been ruined through sexual disease and drug usage is staggering.

Many people confuse license with freedom. True freedom doesn't lie just in the exercise of choices, but in the consequences of the choices as well. You may think you have the freedom to tell a lie, but you will be in bondage to that lie. You will have to remember the nature of the lie and to whom you told it. You may choose to rob a bank, but you will always be looking over your shoulder, fearing you may be caught. License leads to bondage.

If we choose to walk by the flesh, we will have to live with the negative consequences stemming from the choices we make. But living with the consequences of walking by the Spirit is

enabled by the grace manifested in Jesus, who has already suffered for the consequences of our sins.

Walking by the Spirit Is Not Legalism

The second truth we learn from the passage in Galatians is
that walking by the Spirit is not legalism: "If you are led by the
Spirit, you are not under the Law" (5:18). If we choose to relate
to God only by observing the law, however, then we need to be
aware of three other biblical truths.

Law Brings a Curse

First, according to Galatians 3:10-14, the law will function as
a curse:

> All who rely on observing the law are under a
> curse, for it is written: "Cursed is everyone who
> does not continue to do everything written in the
> Book of the Law." Clearly no one is justified before
> God by the law, because, "The righteous will live by
> faith." The law is not based on faith; on the con-
> trary, "The man who does these things will live by
> them." Christ redeemed us from the curse of the law
> by becoming a curse for us, for it is written: "Cursed
> is everyone who is hung on a tree." He redeemed us
> in order that the blessing given to Abraham might
> come to the Gentiles through Christ Jesus, so that by
> faith we might receive the promise of the Spirit
> (NIV).

If we want to base our relationship with God on how well we
keep the law, we should consider James 2:10: "Whoever keeps
the whole law and yet stumbles in one point, he has become
guilty of all." Thankfully, our relationship with God is based on
our identity and position in Christ, not on our ability to keep
the law. We are not saved by how we perform, we are saved and

sanctified by what we have chosen to believe: "The law has become our tutor to lead us to Christ, so that we may be justified by faith" (Galatians 3:24). The blessings of Abraham have come to the Gentiles, and every born-again believer is alive in Christ Jesus.

We are no longer under the Old Covenant of law. We are under the New Covenant of grace. Christianity is not trying to live according to the law as best as we can. Christianity is living by faith, according to what God says is true, in the power of the Holy Spirit. "He redeemed us in order that the blessing given to Abraham might come to the Gentiles through Christ Jesus, so that by faith we might receive the promise of the Spirit" (Galatians 3:14 NIV).

Many Christians labor in the fog of legalism. It is like they have never heard the good news of the gospel. Going to a legalistic church is bad news. Such churches motivate by guilt, even though there is no condemnation for those who are in Christ Jesus (Romans 8:1). Legalistic pastors instill fear in the hearts of believers, but "God has not given us a spirit of timidity, but of power and love and discipline" (2 Timothy 1:7). As a pastor, I also desire that God's children live righteous lives, but they can't do this by living under law. Under the New Covenant of grace, we actually can live up to the standards of God's moral law by faith in the power of the Holy Spirit.

Law Cannot Give Life

The second limitation of law is that it is powerless to give life. Telling people that what they are doing is wrong does not give them the power to stop. "Is the law then contrary to the promises of God? May it never be! For if a law had been given which was able to impart life, then righteousness would indeed have been based on law" (Galatians 3:21).

We were dead in our trespasses and sins, but now we are alive *in Christ*—we are "servants of a new covenant, not of the letter but of the Spirit; for the letter kills, but the Spirit gives life" (2 Corinthians 3:6). This life establishes our true identity as children of God. Jesus said, "I came that they may have life, and have it abundantly" (John 10:10).

The New Testament writers are trying to teach us that we are children of God (John 1:12), and the Holy Spirit is bearing witness with our spirit that we are children of God (Romans 8:16). Knowing who we are in Christ affects the way we live. "See how great a love the Father has bestowed on us, that we would be called children of God; and such we are...And everyone who has this hope fixed on Him purifies himself, just as He is pure" (1 John 3:1,3).

We cannot consistently behave in a way that is inconsistent with what we believe about ourselves. But we are not just forgiven sinners. We are new creations in Christ (2 Corinthians 5:17). We are "saints by calling, with all who in every place call on the name of the Lord Jesus Christ, their Lord and ours" (1 Corinthians 1:2). God has changed who we are, but it is our responsibility to live in accordance with this.

Law Stimulates Sinful Desires

Law has a third limitation. It actually has the capacity to stimulate the desire to do that which it was intended to prohibit. According to Paul, the law actually arouses our sinful passions. "While we were in the flesh, the sinful passions, which were aroused by the law, were at work in the members of our body to bear fruit for death." Is the law sinful then? Not according to Paul's words in Romans 7:7-8:

> Is the Law sin? May it never be! On the contrary, I would not have come to know sin except through the Law; for I would not have known about coveting if the Law had not said, "You shall not covet." But sin, taking opportunity through the commandment, produced in me coveting of every kind; for apart from the Law sin is dead.

If you don't believe that the law has this capacity, then try telling your children they can go one place but not another. The moment you say that, where do they want to go? The forbidden fruit seems to be the most desirable. When I was young, I had some friends who were Roman Catholic. Their parish posted a list of movies they couldn't see...which quickly became a list of movies to see. Those were the "good" ones! My friends actually tore the list off the wall of the church and shared it with everyone they knew.

I'm not suggesting that we don't need or don't have a moral standard! Of course we need a moral standard, for without it we wouldn't come to Christ. But now that we are in Christ, the law is no longer the means by which we live a righteous life.

Walking in Balance

The Holy Spirit will enable us to walk between the two extremes of legalism and license. The Christian life is like a journey up a mountain road. The Holy Spirit provides sanctuary for those who walk the narrow path. To the right of the path is a cliff. It is too steep to climb and too far down to jump. It is a tempting choice, however. You could sail off that cliff and enjoy an exhilarating "flight." But that choice has serious consequences—like the sudden stop at the end! Succumbing to the desires of the flesh, doing as I please, and demanding my "right" of freedom of choice without considering the consequences is license. It's a deadly step in the wrong direction.

To the left of that road is a roaring fire. The "accuser of the brethren" has a field day with those who choose to deviate from the narrow path by reverting to the law. Many Christians are burned by legalism. Some become perfectionists, trying desperately to live up to the law. Others feel so condemned by their failures that they stay away from churches and friends who they feel may be inclined to put another guilt trip on them. Paul warned us, "It was for freedom that Christ set us free; therefore keep standing firm and do not be subject again to a yoke of slavery" (Galatians 5:1).

The devil is a tempter. He wants us to jump off that cliff. "Go on and do it. Everybody's doing it. You'll get away with it. Who would know? You know you want to." As soon as you give into the temptation, his role changes from tempter to accuser. "You're sick. And you call yourself a Christian. You'll never get away with this. God can't possibly love such a miserable failure as you."

So if walking by the Spirit is not license, and it's not legalism, then what is it? It is liberty: "Now the Lord is the Spirit, and where the Spirit of the Lord is, there is liberty" (2 Corinthians 3:17). Let us consider next how we can experience this liberated walk with God.

Walking with God

There are two other boundaries that we have to consider before we can say we have an understanding of what it means to walk free in Christ. First, walking by the Spirit is not sitting passively, expecting God to do everything for us. Second, walking by the Spirit is not running around in endless, exhausting activities as though everything depended on our efforts. How much gets accomplished for the kingdom of God if we expect God to do everything without us? Nothing! It is the eternal purpose of God to make His wisdom known through the church (Ephesians 3:8-11). How much gets accomplished for the kingdom of God if we try to do it all by ourselves? Jesus said, "Apart from Me you can do nothing" (John 15:5). If there is no watering or planting, then nothing grows. We have the privilege to water and plant, but God causes the increase.

There was a pastor whose favorite hobby was gardening. One day a neighbor walked by and said, "The Lord sure gave you a beautiful garden." The pastor responded, "This garden belongs to the Lord, and I have the privilege to tend it. But you should have seen this plot of ground when the Lord had it all to Himself."

Taking on Jesus' Yoke

Responding to Pharisaic legalism, Jesus said, "Come to Me, all who are weary and heavy-laden, and I will give you rest. Take My yoke upon you and learn from Me, for I am gentle and humble in heart, and you will find rest for your souls. For my yoke is easy and my burden is light" (Matthew 11:28-30). Jesus was a carpenter in His youth, but carpenters didn't frame houses as they do today. They fashioned yokes and doors, both of which Jesus would use as metaphors of Himself.

A yoke harnessed two oxen together. When a young ox was being broken in, it was paired with a lead ox. Having had much training, the lead ox already knew the best way to accomplish a day's work. If he walked a steady even pace, he wouldn't burn out before noon. He had also learned to look neither to the left nor to the right. He had learned to pull together when yoked with another ox, which was the only way the two were going to accomplish anything.

Young oxen get impatient with the slow pace and want to run ahead. Do you know what they get? A sore neck! Other young oxen feel like doing nothing and just want to sit. Guess what they get? A sore neck. The lead ox is going to keep right on walking no matter what the young ox does, because he is listening to his master. Whether we sit down or drop out, life goes on. When we are yoked with Jesus, our lead ox, He will maintain a steady pace right down the center of the narrow path.

When my children were little, we had a perfect family dog. When little Missy died, it was traumatic for all of us. I hurried to a pet store the same day and bought a replacement dog. This was like a disastrous marriage on the rebound. Buster grew up to be a DAWG! He was the most neurotic mess I've ever seen. My son signed him up for 12 lessons at a dog-obedience class, but after two weeks he gave up.

One day I decided to give Buster a lesson in walking with his master. So I put a choke chain around his neck, and we went for a walk. I was the master in this relationship, and I knew where I wanted to walk. I said walk—not run! That dumb dog nearly choked himself to death trying to run. When Buster stopped to sniff a flower or some gross thing, I kept on walking, determined to teach that dog to walk by his master. Then he would stray off the path and end up winding his leash around a tree. As I kept on walking, the result was like a wild ride at an amusement park. You ask, "Did that dumb dog ever learn to walk obediently by his master?" No, he never did. I've known a few Christians who haven't either.

Jesus said, "Come to Me. I'm the lead ox. Are you weary and heavy-laden? I'll give you rest. Take My yoke." The flesh responds, "That's all I need—another yoke!" But when you put on the yoke of Christ, you must throw off the yokes of legalism and license. Jesus may be our crutch, but He is the only one we need. "Learn from Me," Jesus said. What would we learn if we walked with Jesus? We would learn to take one day at a time. We would learn the priority of relationship. We would learn that our walk is one of faith, not sight, and one of grace, not legalism.

Jesus said, "My yoke is easy and My burden is light." If we find ourselves huffing and puffing our way through life, maybe we're not walking with God. Maybe we're running in the flesh. We may look back over the years and say, "We did this and we did that. We went here and we went there." But how much fruit remains? We don't measure our spirituality by our activities— we measure it by the fruit of righteousness and reproduction.

This passage in Matthew is the only place in the New Testament where Jesus described Himself. He said, "I am gentle and humble in heart." We have been invited to walk with the gentle Jesus. Imagine that! "Therefore as you have received Christ Jesus the Lord, so walk in Him" (Colossians 2:6).

Following Our Guide

The Holy Spirit also leads us. Being led by the Spirit is defined by two boundaries as well. First, the Holy Spirit is not pushing us. Motivated by guilt, many Christians can't seem to say "no." They expend a lot of energy, but they bear very little fruit. They measure success in ministry by the number of activities, and spirituality by the expenditure of human energy. There is a major difference between being called into ministry and being driven to perform. The latter leads to burnout.

Second, we are not being lured away by the Holy Spirit. If you are being pressured to make a hasty decision, just say "no"— because God doesn't lead that way. The devil does. He demands an answer right now and withdraws the offer if time for consideration is requested. The guidance of God may come suddenly, but it never comes to the spiritually unprepared. Pentecost was sudden, but the disciples had spent days in prayerful preparation.

Many believers are lured away by various impulses. The lure of knowledge and power is the most common trap. These Christians don't seem to understand that they already have all the power they need in Christ (Ephesians 1:18-19). What we all need is truth, and if we learn to pray by the Spirit, He will lead us into all truth.

Some believers are easily lured away because they have not exercised any spiritual discipline. They don't study and they don't pray. They want an air-traffic controller to explain the instruction manual to them while they are in the air. Why study when you can receive guidance from your "spirit guide" or from some other "spiritual teacher" who will study for you? We have been warned about such spiritual laziness in 2 Timothy 3:1-7:

> Realize this, that in the last days difficult times will come. For men will be lovers of self, lovers of money, boastful, arrogant, revilers, disobedient to parents, ungrateful, unholy, unloving, irreconcilable, malicious gossips, without self-control, brutal,

haters of good, treacherous, reckless, conceited, lovers of pleasure rather than lovers of God, holding to a form of godliness, although they have denied its power; Avoid such men as these. For among them are those who enter into households and captivate weak women weighed down with sins, led on by various impulses, always learning and never able to come to the knowledge of the truth.

Growing up on a farm, I had the privilege to raise championship stock sheep. I can tell you from experience that sheep are not the smartest animals on the farm. They're right down there with chickens. For instance, you can self-feed cattle and pigs, but you can't do this with sheep. If you turn sheep loose in a green pasture without a shepherd, they will literally eat themselves to death. I believe that is why the Shepherd "makes me lie down in green pastures" (Psalm 23:2).

In the Western world, we drive sheep from the rear. The Australians use sheepdogs, which is similar. However, that is not the case in Israel. In my trips to the Holy Land, I have observed shepherds sitting patiently while the flock feeds on the grass. When an area is sufficiently grazed, the shepherd will say something and walk off. The sheep look up and follow him. What a beautiful illustration of what the Lord said in John 10:27: "My sheep hear My voice, and I know them, and they follow Me."

Walking by the Spirit is neither legalism nor license. It's not sitting passively, waiting for God to do something, nor is it running around in endless activities trying to accomplish something by our own strength and resources. If we walk by the Spirit, we are neither driven nor lured off the path of faith, "for all who are being led by the Spirit of God, these are sons of God" (Romans 8:14). Why would someone want a "spirit guide" when they could have the Holy Spirit as their guide?

QUESTIONS FOR THOUGHT AND DISCUSSION

1. What were the two key elements ensuring the safe landing of the young pilot in the opening illustration?

   a. Knowledge of _____

   b. Faith in _____

2. How did the early church discover the mind of Christ?

3. Why has simply preaching morality not changed our society?

4. What excesses are seen among those who consider freedom a license to do whatever they want?

5. What does legalism accomplish, and why is the law ineffective?

6. Has laying down the law in your church, home, or society ever stimulated you to do what it is intended to prohibit?

7. Which side of the road represents your greatest weakness—legalism or license? How can you stay in the center of the road?

8. What would you learn if you walked with Jesus?

9. How did Jesus describe Himself?

10. How does the Holy Spirit's guidance come or not come, and who can expect to be guided?

11. What steps can you take to be more sensitive to the Holy Spirit's guidance in your life?

CHAPTER SIX

When Heaven Is Silent

*If I could hear Christ praying for me in the next
room, I would not fear a million enemies.
Yet distance makes no difference. He is praying for me.*

ROBERT MURRAY M'CHEYNE

BEING LED BY THE HOLY SPIRIT and living in His power is a liberating experience for every child of God. Sensing His presence, living victoriously, and knowing the truth are characteristics of a free person. But what if you couldn't sense His presence? What if you hadn't heard from God and it seemed your prayers were not being answered? What if God, for some reason, suspended His conscious blessings? What would you do if you were faithfully walking in the light and suddenly you found yourself engulfed in darkness?

Job was enjoying the benefits of living righteously when, unexpectedly, it was all taken away. Health, wealth, and family were all gone! If we found ourselves in Job's shoes, our minds would likely spin with many questions:

"What did I do to deserve this?"

"Did I miss a turn in the road?"

"Is this what I get for living a righteous life?"

"Where is God?"

"God, why are You doing this to me?"

Like Job, we might even feel like cursing the day we were born.

My family and I have been through two dark periods in our lives, both of which preceded significant changes in my ministry. There were days when I wasn't sure if we were going to make it. Heaven was silent for weeks and months. I'm not sure we would have survived those trials if it weren't for the message given in Isaiah 50:10-11:

> Who is among you that fears the LORD, that obeys the voice of His servant, that walks in darkness and has no light? Let him trust in the name of the LORD and rely on his God. Behold, all you who kindle a fire, who encircle yourselves with firebrands, walk in the light of your fire and among the brands you have set ablaze. This you will have from My hand: and you will lie down in torment.

"Who is among you that fears the LORD?" Isaiah is talking about a believer—somebody who obeys God and yet walks in darkness. Isaiah is not talking about the darkness of sin or even the darkness of this world (that is, the kingdom of darkness). He's talking about the darkness of uncertainty, a heavy blanket of dark cloud that hovers over our very being. The certainties of yesterday have been replaced by the uncertainties of tomorrow. God has suspended His conscious blessings. Even attending church may seem like a dismal experience. Friends seem more like a bother than a blessing. Can this happen to a true believer? What is God trying to accomplish with His "ministry of darkness"? What is a person to do during these times?

Keep On Walking in the Light
of Previous Revelation

First, the passage tells us that we are to keep on walking. When we were in the light we could see the next step—the path ahead was clear. We knew a friend from an enemy, and we could see where the obstacles were. The Word was a lamp for our feet, it directed our steps—but now we begin to wonder if it's true. Darkness has overcome us. We are embarrassed by how disoriented we feel. Every natural instinct says, "Drop out, sit down, stop!" But the Bible encourages us to keep on living by faith according to what we know to be true.

Our First Testing

Our family's first encounter with such a period of darkness came after my wife, Joanne, discovered that she was developing cataracts in both eyes. In the late 1970s they would not do lens implants for anybody under the age of 60. We had no alternative but to watch each of her eyes cloud over until she could barely see. Then they surgically removed her lenses. Thick cataract glasses were prescribed until Joanne could be fitted with contact lenses. Her traumatic experience lasted for two years.

Living as a pastor's wife is pressure enough, but this additional difficulty was a burden that was too heavy. So for Joanne's sake, I started to consider another way to serve the Lord besides being a senior pastor. At the time I sensed God leading me to pursue my first doctoral degree, even though I had no idea what He had in store for me. Just the assurance that I was putting her ahead of my desire to pastor a church gave Joanne a sense of hope. However, since our church was in the middle of a building program, I needed to stay until the project was complete. But within months after we dedicated our new buildings, God released me from that pastorate.

I was nearing the completion of my doctoral studies and was facing the major task of doing research and writing my dissertation. I also wanted to finish a second seminary degree. Sensing God's release, I began one of the most difficult educational years of my life. In one year I completed 43 semester units, 17 of which were language studies in Greek and Hebrew. In the middle of that year I took my comprehensive exams, and by the end of the year I finished my research and wrote my doctoral dissertation. I also taught part-time at Talbot School of Theology. It was a difficult year to say the least. If you take a year off for education with very little income, you try to accomplish as much as you possibly can.

We had started that year with the assurance that $20,000 would be made available to us interest-free. Our plan was to pay off the loan when we sold our home in the future. Not having to sell our house right then allowed us to keep our children in the same school for that year. I was confident that God would have a place for us after I had completed my education. So with the first half of the $20,000 in hand, I proceeded in the anticipation of finishing my doctorate and a second master's degree. For the next six months our life unfolded as planned—then God turned out the lights.

Apparently the second half of the promised $20,000 wasn't going to come in. Since we had no other source of income, our cupboards became bare. I had no job, and my educational goals were only half completed. I had always considered myself a faithful person, but now I was on the brink of not being able to provide for the basic needs of my family. I had been so certain of God's calling six months earlier, but now the darkness of uncertainty had settled in.

Doubts Come In

It all culminated two weeks before my comprehensive exams, which took place on two consecutive Saturdays. Only 10 percent of the doctoral candidates had passed the previous testing. So I was facing a lot of pressure. If I didn't pass the exams, I couldn't start my research and dissertation. I had already invested three years of my life and $15,000 in the program. Now we didn't even know where our next meal was coming from. We had equity in our home, but at the time interest rates were so high that houses weren't selling. The temptation to create my own light was almost overwhelming. I looked into a couple of ministry opportunities, but I knew they weren't for me—and I couldn't accept them. The problem wasn't pride or an unwillingness to work—I would have sold hot dogs to provide for my family. I just wanted God's guidance, and He wasn't giving it to me!

I began to wonder if I had made the wrong decision. God's leading had been so clear the past summer. Why was I walking in darkness now? It was as though God had dropped me into a funnel, and it was getting darker and darker. When I thought it couldn't get much darker, I hit the narrow part! Then at the darkest hour God dropped us out of the bottom of that funnel, and everything became clear again. I can say from experience that it is always the darkest before the dawn.

The Lord Speaks

It was early on a Thursday morning, in the middle of my sleep, when the dawn broke. Nothing changed circumstantially, but everything changed internally. I remember waking up with a sense of joy. My wife also awoke, startled, and wondered what was going on—but she too could sense that something was taking place. I had a conscious awareness of God in a remarkable way. No audible voices or visions, but I was clearly hearing from heaven. God in His quiet and gentle way was renewing my mind. The essence of my thought process went like this: "Neil, do you walk by faith, or do you walk by sight? Are you walking by faith now? You believed Me last summer—do you believe Me now? Neil, do you love Me, or do you love My blessings? Do you worship Me for who I am, or do you worship Me for the blessings I bring? What if I suspended My conscious presence in your life—would you still trust Me?"

I learned something that morning in a way I had never experienced before. In my spirit I responded, "Lord, you know I love You, and of course I walk by faith, not by sight. Lord, I worship You because of who You are, and I know that You will never leave me or forsake me. Lord, I confess that I doubted Your place in my life and questioned Your ability to provide for all our needs."

Those precious moments can't be planned or predicted. They're never repeatable. During those times, what we have previously learned from the Bible becomes deeply imbedded in our hearts. Our worship is purified, and our love clarified. Faith moves from a textbook principle to a living reality. Trust is deepened when God puts us in a position where we have no other choice but to trust Him. We either learn to trust Him during these times...or we end up compromising our faith and walk away from God. The Bible gives us the only infallible rules of faith and the only knowledge of the Object of our faith, but we learn to *live* by faith in the course of life. This is especially true when circumstances are not working favorably for us. The Lord has a way of stretching us through a knothole—and just before we are about to break in half, suddenly we slip through to the other side. But we will never go back to the same shape we were before.

Outward Change Follows Inward Change

Later that day everything changed. The dean at Talbot School of Theology called to ask if I had taken another position. He asked me not to accept anything until we had the opportunity to talk. That afternoon he offered me the position I held for the next ten years. Friday evening, a man from my previous ministry stopped by at 10 P.M. When I asked him what he was doing at our home at that hour of the night, he said he wasn't sure. I invited him in with the promise that we would figure out something. I half-jokingly asked him if he'd like to buy my house—and he responded, "Maybe I would." The next Tuesday he and his parents made an offer on our house, which we accepted. Now we could sell our house because we knew the destination of our next move.

Nothing had changed externally before that morning, but everything had changed internally. God can change in a moment what circumstances can never change. My wife and I had previously made the following commitment which helped sustain us during this time and others: "We will never make a major decision when we are down." That alone has kept me from resigning my position after difficult board meetings or messages that bombed. The point is, never doubt in darkness what God has clearly shown you in the light. We are to keep on walking in the light of previous revelation. If it was true six months ago, it's still true now. If we're serious about our walk with God, He will test us to determine if we love Him or His blessings. He may cloud the future so we learn to walk by faith and not by sight or feelings.

Understand that God has not left us—He has only suspended His "conscious" presence so that our faith will never rest on our feelings, or be established by unique experiences, or be fostered by blessings. If our earthly parents were in difficult circumstances and couldn't afford any Christmas presents when we were young, would we stop loving them? Would we stop looking to them for direction and support? If God's "ministry of darkness" should envelop you, keep on walking in the light of previous revelation.

Don't Create Your Own Light

"Don't light your own fire" is the second lesson we should learn from Isaiah. In other words, don't create your own light. Our natural tendency when we don't see it God's way is to do it our way. Notice the text again: "All you who kindle a fire, who encircle yourselves with firebrands, walk in the light of your fire." God is not talking about the fire of judgment, He's talking about fire that creates light. Notice what happens when people create their own light: "Among the brands you have set ablaze...this you will have from My hand: you will lie down in torment." Essentially God is saying, "Go ahead, do it your way. I will allow it, but misery will follow."

Let me illustrate this principle from the Bible. God called Abraham out of Ur into the Promised Land. In Genesis 12, a covenant was made in which God promised Abraham that his descendants would be more numerous than the sands of the sea or the stars in the sky. Abraham lived his life in the light of that promise—then one day God turned out the light. So many months and years passed that his wife Sarah could no longer bear a child by natural means. God's guidance had been so clear before, but now it looked like Abraham would have to assist God in the fulfillment of His promise. Who could blame Abraham for creating his own light? Sarah supplied the match by offering her handmaiden to Abraham. Out of that union came another nation of people. This has created so much conflict that the whole world lies down in torment, since Jews and Arabs have not been able to dwell together peacefully to this day.

God superintended the birth of Moses and provided for his preservation. Raised in the home of Pharaoh, he was given the second most prominent position in Egypt. But God had put into his heart a burden to set his people free. Attempting to help God set His people free, Moses impulsively pulled out his sword—and God turned out the light. Abandoned to the back side of the desert, Moses spent 40 years tending his father-in-law's sheep. Then one day, Moses turned aside to see a burning bush that wasn't being consumed, and God turned the light back on.

I'm not suggesting that we have to wait 40 years for the cloud to lift. In our life span today, that would be more time than an average person's faith could endure. But the darkness may last for weeks, months, and possibly for some exceptional people, even years. God is in charge, and He knows exactly how small a knothole He can pull us through. Isaiah wrote, "The One forming light and creating darkness, causing well-being and creating calamity; I am the LORD who does all these" (Isaiah 45:7).

Darkness Again

Let me share our second period of darkness. Five years after Joanne's surgery to remove the lenses in both of her eyes, her doctor suggested that she have lens implants. So much scientific progress had been made that implant surgery had become a simple outpatient procedure. At first Joanne was reluctant—and our insurance wouldn't pay, calling the surgery cosmetic. Finally they came around, and then Joanne's doctor and I convinced her that it was the best thing to do.

Having someone cut into your eyeball is not something you look forward to. Just the thought of it can send shivers down your spine. So Joanne's emotional state before surgery was somewhat troubled, which is understandable. But even though the operation was successful, Joanne emerged from the anesthesia in a phobic state. She had been anesthetized during surgery before, so I couldn't understand why she was so fearful now. Could the anesthetic itself have caused her emotional state? Or could the nature of her postoperative care been a factor? The cost of medical care has pushed many hospitals into day surgeries that leave no time for rest or recovery.

The nurses had to ask for my assistance in helping Joanne come out of the anesthesia. They needed to clear the bed because Joanne was just one of several patients that day who would occupy the small recovery room. Some people need more emotional care than that. Perhaps if she had been permitted to recover gradually from her experience and spend at least one night in the hospital, she might have done much better. But bringing Joanne home that afternoon was an ordeal for both of us. She just couldn't stabilize emotionally.

The possibility of this situation also being a spiritual battle became evident the next day. Joanne thought she had a foreign object in her that had to come out. This made no rational sense to me, since the surgery had been successful. She could see with 20/30 vision. However, I didn't understand the battle for our minds then as I do today. For instance, I have seen young women who struggle with eating disorders suffer from similar thoughts. Paul said, "I find...the principle that evil is present in me, the one who wants to do good" (Romans 7:21). These young women believe they have evil present in them and they have to get it out. Their vomiting, defecating, or cutting themselves is based on a lie: that the evil is in their blood, feces, or food. Just as with these others, the evil that Joanne was fighting was not the physical kind—it was the lie of Satan coming at a very vulnerable moment.

It is painful to recall this because much of what followed could have been avoided. (I believe every Christian should pray and be prayed for before every surgery.) Joanne's struggle with anxiety led to sleeplessness and finally, depression. She went from her eye doctor, to her primary care doctor, to her gynecologist, and finally to a psychiatrist. Since none of them could find anything physically wrong with Joanne, they assumed she was a head case or a hormone case. They tried hormones, antidepressants, and sleeping pills, but nothing seemed to work. She lost her appetite, and her weight dropped significantly. She was hospitalized five times.

This Too Will Pass

Getting proper medical help was exceedingly expensive. Our insurance ran out, and we had to sell our house to pay the medical bills. For months, Joanne couldn't function as a mother or wife. My daughter wasn't sure if she could handle it if her mother were to die. My son withdrew into himself. I got caught in a role conflict like never before. Was I Joanne's pastor, counselor, discipler...or was I supposed to be just her husband? I decided there was only one role I could fulfill in her life, and that was to be her husband. If someone was going to fix my wife, it would have to be someone other than me. My role was to hold her every day and say, "Joanne, this too will pass."

I was thinking it would be a matter of weeks, but it turned into a 15-month-long ordeal. The funnel got narrower and narrower. During this time the words of Isaiah 21:11-12 had great meaning for me:

> One keeps calling to me from Seir, "Watchman,
> how far gone is the night? Watchman, how far gone
> is the night?" The watchman says, "Morning comes
> but also night."

A ministry of hope must be based on the truth that "morning comes." No matter how dark the night...morning comes. In our darkest hour, when I wasn't even sure if Joanne was going to live or die...morning came. Joanne had all but given up any medical hope, but then a doctor in private practice was recommended to her. He immediately took Joanne off the medication she was on and prescribed a much more balanced approach, one that dealt with her depression but also with her general health, including nutrition.

At the same time we had a day of prayer at Biola University where I was teaching. I had nothing to do with events of the day other than to set aside special time for prayer in my own classes. That evening, the undergraduate students had a communion service. Since I taught at the graduate level, I normally wouldn't have gone, but work had detained me on campus, so I decided to participate. I sat on the gym floor with the students and took communion. I'm sure nobody in the student body was aware that it was one of the loneliest and darkest times of my life. I was deeply committed to doing God's will, and I was walking as best I could in the light of previous revelation, but I felt incredibly lonely and frustrated. There was nothing I could do to change Joanne or the circumstances.

Morning Comes

I can honestly say I never once questioned God or felt bitter about my circumstances—and I have Him to thank for sustaining me. For some time, the Lord had been preparing my heart and leading me into a ministry to bind up the brokenhearted and set captives free. Somehow I knew that the nature of my ministry was related to what my family was going through, but I didn't know what to do about it. Should I abandon what I was doing to help others in order to spare my family? God was blessing my ministry in unprecedented ways, but my family wasn't being blessed. He had stripped us of everything we owned. All we had left was each other and our relationship with Him. But when God is all you have, you began to discover that God is all you need. When we had exhausted all our resources, morning came!

If God has ever spoken to my heart, He did in that communion service. There were no voices or visions. It was just His quiet and gentle way of renewing my mind—the same way He renews all our minds. It didn't come by way of the worship leader's message or the testimonies of the students—but it did come in the context of taking communion. The essence of my thoughts were as follows: "Neil, there's a price to pay for freedom. It cost My Son His life. Are you willing to pay the price?" "Dear God, if that's the reason, I'm willing—but if it's some stupid thing I'm doing, then I pray that You would tell me," I responded. I left that evening with the inward assurance that it was over. The circumstances hadn't changed, but in my heart I knew that morning had come.

Within a week Joanne woke up one morning and said, "Neil, I slept last night." From that point on she knew she was on the road to recovery. She never looked back, but continued on to full and complete recovery. At the same time our ministry took a quantum leap. What was the point of all this? Why did we have to go through such a trial?

Brokenness: the Key to Ministry

There are several reasons why God takes some of His children through His ministry of darkness. First, *we learn a lot about ourselves* during those times. In my case, whatever was left of my flesh that gave simplistic "advice" such as "Why don't you read your Bible?" or "Just work harder" or "Pray more" was mercifully stripped away. Most people going through dark times want to do the right thing, but many can't—or at least don't believe they can—and they don't know why. In such times we realize our limitations and deepen our roots in the eternal streams of life, while we sever our ties to temporal answers and props that don't last.

Second, during God's ministry of darkness *we learn compassion*. We learn to wait patiently with people. We learn to weep with those who weep, not instruct them. We learn to respond to the emotional needs of people who have lost hope. Instruction will come when it is appropriate. I believe that I was a caring person before—but nothing like I am now because of God's gracious way of ministering to me.

We had some "friends," like those who tried to help Job, advise us in our time of darkness—and I can tell you it hurts. What Job needed in his hour of darkness was a few good friends who would just sit with him. This they did for one week, and then their patience ran out. In our situation, the meaningful help we received was from the church—people who just stood by us and prayed. As Christians we have to ask ourselves, if God took away every material blessing and reduced our assets to nothing more than meaningful relationships, would that be enough for us?

Third, *we learn contentment*. Most of the world has learned to be content with food and clothing because they have no other choice. Paul said, "I know how to get along with humble means, and I also know how to live in prosperity; in any and every circumstance I have learned the secret of being filled and going hungry, both of having abundance and suffering need" (Philippians 4:12). That is an important lesson to learn.

Fourth, *we learn to be confident that God makes everything right in the end*. The final lot of Job was far better than it was at the beginning. The same happened for us. Within two years God replaced everything we lost, and it was far better, in terms of home, family, and ministry.

Fifth, I believe that God brings us to the end of our resources in order that *we may learn to discover His resources*. We don't hear enough sermons on brokenness these days. It's the great omission—and that's why we can't fulfill the great commission. In all four Gospels, Jesus taught us to deny ourselves, pick up our cross daily, and follow Him. When it was time for Him to be glorified, He said, "Truly, truly, I say to you, unless a grain of wheat falls into the ground and dies, it remains alone; but if it dies, it bears much fruit" (John 12:24).

I don't know of any painless way to die to self-rule. Self-sufficiency is the biggest obstacle to overcome if we are going to find our sufficiency in Christ. I do know that denying self is necessary and that it's the best possible thing that could ever happen to us. "We who live are constantly being delivered over to death for Jesus' sake, so that the life of Jesus also may be manifested in our mortal flesh" (2 Corinthians 4:11).

Joseph was no good for God in Potiphar's house. God had to strip him of his earthly possessions and positions before he could be an instrument in God's hand. Chuck Colson was no good for God in the White House, but he became a powerful force in prison. I had a lot of hard-earned qualifications, including five degrees, but I wasn't much good for God until I suffered the loss of all things.

I know now that I can't set a captive free or bind up the brokenhearted, but God can. Every book I have written and every tape I have recorded have all been after this experience. That period of brokenness was the beginning of Freedom in Christ Ministries, which has spread all over the world. "No pain, no gain," says the bodybuilder. That is also true in the spiritual realm. Remember Isaiah's second point: Don't create your own light. Man-made light is very deceptive.

A Lesson in Trust

The final point Isaiah makes is, "Let him trust in the name of the LORD and rely on his God" (50:10). Walking in darkness is a lesson in trust. Every great period of personal growth in my own life and ministry has been preceded by a major time of testing. As I've mentioned, the first led to my appointment to teach at Talbot School of Theology, and the second led to the birth of Freedom in Christ Ministries.

Possibly the greatest sign of spiritual maturity is the ability to postpone rewards. The ultimate test for us would be to receive nothing in this lifetime while continuing to look forward to receiving our reward in the life to come. This was true for the heroes of Hebrews 11:

> All these died in faith without receiving the promises, but having seen them and having welcomed them from a distance, and having confessed that they were strangers and exiles on this earth. For those who say such things make it clear that they are seeking a country of their own (verse 13).

And then verse 39 reads,

> All these, having gained approval through their faith, did not receive what was promised, because God had provided something better for us, so that apart from us they would not be made perfect.

If I had known beforehand what my family would have to go through to get where we are today, I probably wouldn't have come. But looking back, we can all say, "We're glad we came." That's the reason God doesn't show us what's on the other side of the door. Remember, He makes everything right in the end. Though it may not be in this lifetime, as it wasn't for those mentioned in Hebrews 11, I believe with all my heart that when life is done and we look back, we will all say that the will of God is good, acceptable, and perfect.

> It is not the critic who counts, nor the man who points how the strong man stumbled, or where the doer of deeds could have done better. The credit

belongs to the man who is actually in the arena, whose face is marred by the dust and sweat and blood; who strives valiantly; who errs and comes short again and again; who knows the great enthusiasms, the great devotions, and spends himself in a worthy cause; who, at best, knows in the end the triumph of high achievement; and who, at the worst, if he fails, at least fails while daring greatly, so that his place shall never be with those cold and timid souls who know neither victory or defeat.

—Theodore Roosevelt

We are in the arena of life, but we don't have to fear the outcome of the battle. We can say that with confidence. The battle is not ours; it is the Lord's. We have His truth, and He has made every provision for us. Satan has no place in our lives. The Holy Spirit is guiding us and protecting us. May the Lord continue to fill you with the knowledge of His will.

Questions for Thought and Discussion

1. What are three characteristics of a free person?

2. Have you recently gone through or are you now going through, a "Job" experience? What feelings does that arouse in you?

3. If the assurances of yesterday have been replaced by the uncertainties of tomorrow, how can you get back to the assurances of God?

4. Have you ever doubted in darkness what God has clearly shown you in the light? What will enable you to keep on walking in the light of previous revelation?

5. Based on the experiences of Abraham and Moses, what may be some of the consequences of creating our own light?

6. What can you expect in the future if you are trying to survive the night?

7. What is the most important lesson to be learned in God's ministry of darkness?

8. If all you had was God, a few friends, and a close family, would that be enough for you?

9. How has the ability to postpone rewards helped you do well in school? Work? Church?

CHAPTER SEVEN

Intimacy with God

*Tell God all that is in your heart, as one unloads
one's heart to a dear friend. People who have
no secrets from each other never want subjects of
conversation; they do not weigh their words,
because there is nothing to be kept back. Neither
do they seek for something to say; they talk out of
the abundance of their hearts, just what they think.
Blessed are they who attain to such familiar,
unreserved intercourse with God.*

FRANÇOIS FENELON

IF YOU DESIRE INTIMACY WITH GOD and a dynamic prayer life,
then the process outlined in this chapter will help you achieve
that objective. The following steps provide an opportunity for
you to have an encounter with God.[5] In each step you will be
submitting to Him and resisting the devil (James 4:7). This
repentance process is a means of resolving personal and spiritual
conflicts that have kept you from having an effective prayer life.
Experiencing your freedom in Christ will be the result of what *you*
choose to believe, confess, forgive, renounce, and forsake. No
one can do that for you.

The Battle for Your Mind

You may experience a battle going on for your mind during the process. However, opposing thoughts cannot have any negative effect upon you unless you believe them. If you experience nagging thoughts like "This isn't going to work" or "God doesn't love me," don't pay attention to them. They will be gone when you are finished.

You will win the battle for your mind as you personally choose the truth, and you will experience your freedom in Christ as God grants repentance. As you go through the process, remember that Satan is under no obligation to obey your thoughts. Only God has complete knowledge of your mind because He alone is omniscient (all-knowing). Find a private place where you can verbally process each step. You can submit to God inwardly, but you need to resist the devil by reading each prayer out loud and by verbally renouncing, forgiving, confessing, and so on.

These steps address critical issues between you and God. You probably will find it possible to process them on your own because Jesus is the Wonderful Counselor. However, some people do need additional help. If you experience difficulty, ask your pastor or a Christ-centered counselor or someone familiar with the Steps to help you.

Both gaining and maintaining your freedom will be greatly enhanced if you read the books *Victory over the Darkness* and *The Bondage Breaker*. They will help you further understand the reality of the spiritual world, your relationship with God, and how to live the Christian life. While the Steps can play a major role in your continuing process of sanctification, there is no such thing as instant maturity. Renewing your mind and being conformed to the image of God are a lifelong process.

Regardless of the source of any difficulty you may have, you have nothing to lose and much to gain by praying through these issues. If your problems stem from a source other than those covered in the Steps, you may need to seek professional help. The real focus in the Steps is your relationship with God. The lack of resolution of any one of these issues will affect your intimacy with Him and your prayer life. "He who conceals his sins does not prosper, but whoever confesses and renounces them finds mercy" (Proverbs 28:13 NIV). Paul wrote, "Since through God's mercy we have this ministry, we do not lose heart. Rather, we have renounced secret and shameful ways; we do not use deception, nor do we distort the word of God" (2 Corinthians 4:1-2 NIV).

Trust God to Lead You

Each Step is explained so you will have no problem knowing what to do. It doesn't make any difference whether or not there are evil spirits present; God is always present and He is all-powerful. If you experience any resistance, stop and pray. If you experience some mental opposition, just ignore it. It is just a thought, and it can have no power over you unless you believe it.

Throughout the process, you will be asking God to lead you. He is the One who grants repentance leading to a knowledge of the truth which sets you free (2 Timothy 2:24-26). Start the Steps with the following prayer and declaration. (It is not necessary to read the words in the parentheses, which are there for clarification or reference.)

Prayer

> *Dear heavenly Father, I acknowledge Your presence in this room and in my life. You are the only omniscient (all-knowing), omnipotent (all-powerful), and omnipresent (always present) God. I am dependent upon You, for apart from You I can do nothing. I stand in the truth that all authority in heaven and on earth has been given to the resurrected Christ, and because I am in Christ, I share that authority in order to make disciples and set captives free. I ask You to fill me with Your Holy Spirit and lead me into all truth. I pray for your complete protection and ask for Your guidance. In Jesus' name I pray, amen.*

Declaration

> *In the name and authority of the Lord Jesus Christ, I command Satan and all evil spirits to release me in order that I can be free to know and to choose to do the will of God. As a child of God who is seated with Christ in the heavenlies, I command every evil spirit to leave my presence. I belong to God, and the evil one cannot touch me.*

Step 1: Counterfeit vs. Real

The first step is to renounce (verbally reject) all past or present involvement with occult practices, cult teachings, and rituals, as well as non-Christian religions. Renounce any activity or group which denies Jesus Christ or offers guidance through any source other than the authority of the Bible. Any group that requires secret initiations, dark ceremonies, or pacts should also be renounced. Begin this step by praying aloud,

> *Dear heavenly Father, I ask You to bring to my mind anything and everything that I have done knowingly or unknowingly that involves occult, cult, or non-Christian teachings or practices. I want to experience Your freedom by renouncing all counterfeit teachings and practices. In Jesus' name I pray, amen.*

Even if you took part in something and thought it was just a game or a joke, you need to renounce it. Satan will try to take advantage of anything he can in our lives, so it is always wise to be as thorough as possible. Even if you were just standing by and watching others do it, you need to renounce your passive involvement. You may not have even realized at the time that what was going on was evil. Still, you should renounce it.

If something comes to your mind and you are not sure what to do about it, trust that the Holy Spirit is answering your prayer, and renounce it.

The following "Non-Christian Spiritual Checklist" covers many of the common occult, cult, and non-Christian religious groups and practices. It is not a complete list, however. God may enable you to recall other experiences not listed that you were personally involved with.

After the checklist, there are some additional questions designed to help you become aware of other things you need to confess and renounce. Below those questions is a short prayer of confession and renunciation. Pray it aloud, filling in the blanks with the groups, teachings, or practices that the Holy Spirit has prompted you to renounce during this time of personal evaluation.

Non-Christian Spiritual Checklist

(Check all those that you have participated in.)

- ❏ Out-of-body experience (astral projection)
- ❏ Ouija board
- ❏ Bloody Mary
- ❏ Light as a Feather (or other occult games)
- ❏ Table-lifting
- ❏ Magic Eight Ball
- ❏ Spells or curses
- ❏ Mental telepathy or mental control of others
- ❏ Automatic writing
- ❏ Trances
- ❏ Spirit guides
- ❏ Fortune telling or divination (for example, tea leaves)
- ❏ Tarot cards
- ❏ Levitation
- ❏ Magic—The Gathering
- ❏ Witchcraft or sorcery
- ❏ Satanism
- ❏ Palm-reading
- ❏ Astrology or horoscopes
- ❏ Hypnosis
- ❏ Séances

- ❏ Black or white magic
- ❏ Fantasy games with occult images
- ❏ Blood pacts or cutting yourself on purpose
- ❏ Objects of worship, crystals, or good-luck charms
- ❏ Sexual spirits
- ❏ Martial arts (mysticism or devotion to sensei)
- ❏ Superstitions
- ❏ Mormonism (Latter-day Saints)
- ❏ Jehovah's Witness (Watchtower)
- ❏ New Age (books, objects, seminars, medicine)
- ❏ Masons
- ❏ Christian Science
- ❏ Mind-science cults
- ❏ The Way International
- ❏ Unification Church (Moonies)
- ❏ The Forum (est)
- ❏ Church of Scientology
- ❏ Unitarian Universalism
- ❏ The Silva Method (Silva Mind Control)
- ❏ Transcendental meditation (TM)
- ❏ Yoga
- ❏ Hare Krishna
- ❏ Bahaism
- ❏ Native American spirit worship
- ❏ Islam
- ❏ Hinduism
- ❏ Buddhism (including Zen)
- ❏ Black Muslim beliefs
- ❏ Rosicrucianism
- ❏ Occult or violent video, computer and on-line games

1. Have you ever seen, heard, or felt a spiritual being in your room?

2. Do you have recurring nightmares? Specifically renounce any accompanying fear.

3. Do you now have, or have you ever had, an imaginary friend, spirit guide, or "angel" offering you guidance or companionship? (If it has a name, renounce it by name.)

4. Have you ever heard voices in your head or had repeating, nagging thoughts such as "I'm dumb," "I'm ugly," "Nobody loves me," "I can't do anything right"—as if there were a conversation going on inside your head? (List any specific nagging thoughts.)

5. Have you ever consulted a medium, spiritist, or channeler?

6. Have you ever seen or been contacted by beings you thought were aliens?

7. Have you ever made a secret vow or pact (or inner vow, for example, "I will never...")?

8. Have you ever been involved in a satanic ritual of any kind?

9. What other spiritual experiences have you had that were evil, confusing, or frightening?

Once you have completed your checklist and the questions, confess and renounce *each* item you were involved in by praying the following prayer aloud:

> *Lord, I confess I have participated in* _____
> _____, *and I renounce* _____.
> *Thank you that in Christ I am forgiven.*

Step 2: Deception vs. Truth

God's Word is true, and we need to accept His truth in the innermost part of our being (Psalm 51:6). Whether or not we *feel* it is true, we need to *believe* it is true! Jesus is the Truth, the Holy Spirit is the Spirit of truth, and the Word of God is truth—and we are admonished to speak the truth in love (see John 14:6; 16:13; 17:17; Ephesians 4:15).

The believer in Christ should never deceive others by lying, telling "white" lies, exaggerating, stretching the truth, or participating in anything relating to falsehoods. Satan is the father of lies, and he seeks to keep people in bondage through deception. It is the truth in Jesus that sets us free (see John 8:32-36,44; 2 Timothy 2:26; Revelation 12:9). We will find real joy and freedom when we stop living a lie and live openly in the truth. After confessing his sin, King David wrote, "How blessed [happy] is the man...in whose spirit there is no deceit!" (Psalm 32:2).

We have been called to walk in the light (1 John 1:7). When we are sure God loves and accepts us, we can be free to own up to our sins and face reality instead of running and hiding from the truth and painful circumstances.

Start this step by praying the following prayer aloud. Don't let any threatening, opposing thoughts, such as "This is a waste of time" or "I wish I could believe this but I just can't," keep you from praying and choosing the truth. Even if this is difficult for you, keep working your way through. God will strengthen you as you rely on Him.

> *Dear heavenly Father, I know that You want me to know the truth, believe the truth, speak the truth, and live in accordance with the truth. Thank You that it is the truth that will set me free. In many ways I have been deceived by Satan, the father of lies, and I have deceived myself as well.*
>
> *Father, I pray in the name of the Lord Jesus Christ and by virtue of His shed blood and resurrection, asking You to rebuke all evil spirits that are deceiving me.*
>
> *I have trusted in Jesus alone to save me, and so I am Your forgiven child. Therefore, since You accept me just as I am in Christ, I can be free to face my sin and not try to hide. I ask for the Holy Spirit to guide me into all truth. I ask You to "search me, O God, and know my heart; try me and know my anxious thoughts; and see if there be any hurtful way in me, and lead me in the everlasting way." In the name of Jesus, who is the Truth, I pray, amen.*
>
> (See Psalm 139:23-24.)

The following exercise will help you discover ways you may have deceived yourself. Check each area of deception that the Lord brings to your mind and confess it, using the prayer following the list. Remember, you can't instantly renew your mind, but the process won't even get started if you aren't aware of the deception.

Ways to Deceive Yourself

❑ Hearing God's Word but not doing what it says (James 1:22)

❑ Saying I have no sin (1 John 1:8)

❑ Thinking I am something I'm really not (Galatians 6:3)

❑ Thinking I am wise in this worldly age (1 Corinthians 3:18-19)

❑ Thinking I can be truly religious but not bridle my tongue (James 1:26)

> *Lord, I confess that I have deceived myself by _____. Thank You for Your forgiveness. I commit myself to believing only Your truth. In Jesus' name, amen.*

Now that you are alive in Christ, completely forgiven and totally accepted, you don't need to defend yourself the way you used to. Christ is now your defense. Confess the ways the Lord shows you that you have deceived yourself or defended yourself wrongly by using the following lists and prayers of confession:

Ways to Wrongly Defend Yourself

❑ Denial of reality (conscious or unconscious)

❑ Fantasy (escaping reality by daydreaming, TV, movies, music, computer or video games, drugs, alcohol, and so on)

❑ Emotional insulation (withdrawing from people or keeping people at a distance to avoid rejection)

❏ Regression (reverting to less threatening times)

❏ Displaced anger (taking out frustrations on innocent people)

❏ Projection (blaming others for my problems)

❏ Rationalization (making excuses for my own poor behavior)

❏ Lying (presenting a falsehood or a false image)

> *Lord, I confess that I have defended myself wrongly by _____. Thank You for Your forgiveness. I now commit myself to trusting in You to defend and protect me. In Jesus' name, amen.*

Choosing the truth may be hard for you if you have believed lies for many years. You may need some additional counseling to help weed out any defense mechanisms you have relied on to cope with life. Every Christian needs to learn that Christ is the only defense he or she needs. Realizing that you are already forgiven and accepted by God through Christ will help free you up to place all your dependence on Him.

Ways That We Can Be Deceived About God

Sometimes we are greatly hindered from walking by faith in our Father God because of lies we have believed about Him. We are to have a healthy fear of God (awe of His holiness, power, and presence), but we no longer need to fear punishment from Him. Romans 8:15 says, "You have not received a spirit of slavery leading to fear again, but you have received a spirit of adoption as sons by which we cry out, 'Abba! Father!'" The following exercise will help break the chains of those lies and enable you to begin to experience that intimate "Abba, Father" relationship with Him.

Work your way down the lists on the next page item by item, left to right. Begin each statement with the heading in bold at the top of that list. Read through the lists *aloud*.

The Truth About Our Heavenly Father

I renounce the lie that my Father God is...	*I joyfully accept the truth that my Father God is...*
1. distant and uninterested	1. intimate and involved (Psalm 139:1-8)
2. insensitive and uncaring	2. kind and compassionate (Psalm 103:8-14)
3. stern and demanding	3. accepting and filled with joy and love (Zephaniah 3:17; Romans 15:7)
4. passive and cold	4. warm and affectionate (Isaiah 40:11; Hosea 11:3-4)
5. absent or too busy for me	5. always with me and eager to be with me (Jeremiah 31:20; Ezekiel 34:11-16; Hebrews 13:5)
6. never satisfied with what I do, impatient, or angry	6. patient and slow to anger (Exodus 34:6; 2 Peter 3:9)
7. mean, cruel, or abusive	7. loving, gentle, and protective of me (Psalm 18:2; Jeremiah 31:3; Isaiah 42:3)
8. trying to take all the fun out of life	8. trustworthy and wants to give me a full life; His will is good, perfect, and acceptable (Lamentations 3:22-23; John 10:10; Romans 12:1-2)
9. controlling or manipulative	9. full of grace and mercy; He gives me freedom to fail (Luke 15:11-16; Hebrews 4:15-16)
10. condemning or unforgiving	10. tenderhearted and forgiving; His heart and arms are always open to me (Psalm 130:1-4; Luke 15:17-24)
11. nit-picking, exacting, or perfectionistic	11. committed to my growth and proud of me as His growing child (Romans 8:28-29; 2 Corinthians 7:4; Hebrews 12:5-11)

I am the apple of His eye!
(Deuteronomy 32:10 NIV)

Faith Must Be Based on the Truth of God's Word

Faith is the biblical response to the truth, and believing what God says is a choice we all can make. If you say, "I wish I could believe God, but I just can't," you are being deceived. Of course you can believe God, because what God says is always true. Believing is something you choose to do, not something you feel like doing.

Counterfeit spiritualities have twisted the concept of faith by saying that we make something true by believing it. We cannot create reality with our minds. God is the ultimate reality, and only He can create something out of nothing. We *face* reality with our minds, but we don't create it. Faith is choosing to believe and act upon what God says, regardless of feelings or circumstances. Believing something does not make it true. *It's true; therefore, we choose to believe it.*

Just "having faith" is not enough. The key question is whether the object of your faith is trustworthy. If the object of your faith is not reliable, then no amount of believing will work. That is why our faith must be based on the solid rock of God and His Word. Believing God and His Word is the only way to live a responsible and fruitful life.

For generations, Christians have known the importance of publicly declaring what they believe. Read aloud the following "Statement of Truth," thinking about what you are saying. You may find it very helpful to read it daily for several weeks to renew your mind with the truth and replace any lies you have believed.

Statement of Truth

1. *I recognize that there is only one true and living God, who exists as the Father, Son, and Holy Spirit. He is worthy of all honor, praise, and glory as the One who made all things and holds all things together.* (See Exodus 20:2-3; Colossians 1:16-17.)

2. *I recognize that Jesus Christ is the Messiah, the Word who became flesh and dwelt among us. I believe that He came to*

destroy the works of the devil, and that He disarmed the rulers and authorities and made a public display of them, having triumphed over them. (See John 1:1,14; 1 John 3:8; Colossians 2:15.)

3. *I believe that God demonstrated His own love for me in that while I was still a sinner, Christ died for me. I believe that He has delivered me from the domain of darkness and transferred me to His kingdom, and in Him I have redemption, the forgiveness of sins.* (See Romans 5:8; Colossians 1:13-14.)

4. *I believe that I am now a child of God and that I am seated with Christ in the heavenlies. I believe that I was saved by the grace of God through faith, and that it was a gift and not a result of any works on my part.* (See Ephesians 2:6,8-9; 1 John 3:1-3.)

5. *I choose to be strong in the Lord and in the strength of His might. I put no confidence in the flesh, for the weapons of warfare are not of the flesh but are divinely powerful for the destruction of strongholds. I put on the full armor of God. I resolve to stand firm in my faith and resist the evil one.* (See 2 Corinthians 10:4; Ephesians 6:10-20; Philippians 3:3.)

6. *I believe that apart from Christ I can do nothing, so I declare my complete dependence on Him. I choose to abide in Christ in order to bear much fruit and glorify my Father. I announce to Satan that Jesus is my Lord. I reject any and all counterfeit gifts or works of Satan in my life.* (See John 15:5,8; 1 Corinthians 12:3.)

7. *I believe that the truth will set me free and that Jesus is the truth. If He sets me free, I will be free indeed. I recognize that walking in the light is the only path of true fellowship with God and man. Therefore, I stand against all of Satan's deception by taking every thought captive in obedience to Christ. I declare that the Bible is the only authoritative standard for truth and life.* (See John 8:32,36; 14:6; 2 Corinthians 10:5; 2 Timothy 3:15-17; 1 John 1:3-7.)

8. *I choose to present my body to God as a living and holy sacrifice and the members of my body as instruments of righteousness. I choose to renew my mind by the living Word of God in order that I may prove that the will of God is good, acceptable, and perfect. I have put off the old self with its evil practices and have put on the new self. I declare myself to be a new creation in Christ.* (See Romans 6:13; 12:1-2; 2 Corinthians 5:17; Colossians 3:9-10 NIV.)

9. *By faith, I choose to be filled with the Spirit so that I can be guided into all truth. I choose to walk by the Spirit so that I will not carry out the desires of the flesh.* (See John 16:13; Galatians 5:16; Ephesians 5:18.)

10. *I renounce all selfish goals and choose the ultimate goal of love. I choose to obey the two greatest commandments: to love the Lord my God with all my heart, soul, mind, and strength, and to love my neighbor as myself.* (See Matthew 22:37-39; 1 Timothy 1:5.)

11. *I believe that the Lord Jesus has all authority in heaven and on earth, and that He is the head over all rule and authority. I am complete in Him. I believe that Satan and his demons are subject to me in Christ since I am a member of Christ's body. Therefore, I obey the command to submit to God and resist the devil, and I command Satan in the name of Jesus Christ to leave my presence.* (See Matthew 28:18; Ephesians 1:19-23; Colossians 2:10; James 4:7.)

Step 3: Bitterness vs. Forgiveness

We are commanded to get rid of all bitterness in our lives and forgive others as we have been forgiven (Ephesians 4:31-32). Forgiving others is essential for our own freedom and walk with God. Satan will take advantage of us if we don't forgive others from our hearts (2 Corinthians 2:10-11). Ask God to bring to your mind the people you need to forgive by praying the following prayer aloud:

> *Dear heavenly Father, I thank You for the riches of Your kindness, forbearance, and patience toward me, knowing that Your kindness has led me to repentance. I confess that I have not shown that same kindness and patience toward those who have hurt or offended me. Instead, I have held on to my anger, bitterness, and resentment toward them. Please bring to my mind all the people I need to forgive in order that I may now do so. In Jesus' name, amen.*

On a separate sheet of paper, list the names of people who God brings to your mind. At this point don't question whether you need to forgive them or not. If a name comes to mind, just write it down.

Often we hold things against ourselves as well, punishing ourselves for wrong choices we've made in the past. Write "myself" at the bottom of your list if you need to forgive yourself. Forgiving yourself is accepting the truth that God has already forgiven you in Christ. If God forgives you, you can forgive yourself!

Also write down "thoughts against God" at the bottom of your list. Obviously, God has never done anything wrong so we don't have to forgive Him. Sometimes, however, we harbor angry thoughts against Him because He did not do what we wanted Him to do. Those feelings of anger or resentment against God can become a wall between us and Him, so we must let them go.

Before you begin working through the process of forgiving those on your list, take a few minutes to review what forgiveness is and what it is not.

- *Forgiveness is not forgetting.* People who want to forget all that was done to them will find they cannot do it. Don't put off forgiving those who have hurt you, hoping the pain will one day go away. Once you choose to forgive someone, *then* Christ can come and begin to heal you of your hurts. But the healing cannot begin until you first forgive. Forgetting may be a long term by-product of for-giveness, but it is never a means to forgiveness.

- *Forgiveness is a choice, a decision of your will.* Since God requires you to forgive, it is something you can do. Some-times it is hard to forgive someone because we naturally want revenge for the things we have suffered. Forgiveness seems to go against our sense of what is right and fair. So we hold on to our anger, punishing people over and over again in our minds for the pain they've caused us.

  But we are told by God never to take our own revenge (Romans 12:19). Let God deal with the person. Let him or her off your hook because as long as you refuse to for-give someone, you are still hooked to that person. You are still chained to your past, bound up in your bitterness. By forgiving, you let the other person off *your* hook—but he or she is not off *God's* hook. You must trust that God will deal with the person justly and fairly, something you simply cannot do.

  "But you don't know how much this person hurt me!" you might say. You're right. We don't, but Jesus does—and He tells you to forgive others for your sake. Until you let go of your anger and hatred, the person is still hurting you. You can't turn back the clock and change the past, but you can be free from it. You can stop the pain, but there is only one way to do it—forgive from your heart. Forgive others for *your* sake so you can be free from your past.

- *Forgiveness is agreeing to live with the consequences of another person's sin.* That may not seem fair, but we all have to live with the consequences of other people's sins whether we like it or not. The only real choice is to do so in the *bondage of bitterness* or in the *freedom of forgiveness.* If we are to forgive as Christ has forgiven us, we must ask, how did Christ forgive us? He took ours sins upon Himself. When we forgive others we do the same. Where is the justice? The cross makes forgiveness legally and morally right. Jesus died once, for *all* our sins.

Jesus took the *eternal* consequences of sin upon Himself. God "made Him who knew no sin to be sin on our behalf, so that we might become the righteousness of God in Him" (2 Corinthians 5:21). We all suffer the *temporary* consequences of other people's sins, but that is simply a harsh reality of living in a fallen world.

- *Do not wait for the other person to ask for your forgiveness.* Remember, Jesus did not wait for those who were crucifying Him to apologize before He forgave them. Even while they mocked Him and jeered at Him, He prayed, "Father, forgive them; for they do not know what they are doing" (Luke 23:34).

- *Forgive from your heart.* Allow God to bring the painful memories to the surface, and acknowledge how you feel toward those who've hurt you. If your forgiveness doesn't touch the emotional core of your life, it will be incomplete. Too often we're afraid of the pain so we bury our emotions deep down inside us. Let God bring them to the surface so He can begin to heal those damaged emotions.

- *Forgiveness is choosing not to hold someone's sin against him or her anymore.* It is common for bitter people to bring up past issues with those who have hurt them. They want those others to feel as bad as they do! But we must let go of the past and choose to reject any thought of revenge.

  This doesn't mean you continue to put up with the future sins of others. God does not tolerate sin, and neither should you. Don't allow yourself to be continually abused by others. Take a stand against sin while continuing to exercise grace and forgiveness toward those who hurt you. If you need help setting scriptural boundaries to protect yourself from further abuse, talk to a trusted friend, counselor, or pastor.

- *Don't wait until you feel like forgiving.* Then you will never forgive. Make the hard choice to forgive even if you don't feel like it. Once you choose to forgive, Satan will lose his power over you in that area, and God will heal your damaged emotions. *Freedom* is what you will gain right now, not necessarily an immediate change in feelings.

Now you are ready to begin. Starting with the first person on your list, make the choice to forgive him or her for every painful memory that comes to your mind. Stay with that individual until you are sure you have dealt with all the remembered pain. Then work your way down the list in the same way.

As you begin forgiving people, God may bring to your mind painful memories you've totally forgotten. Let Him do this even if it hurts. God wants you to be free; forgiving those people is the only way. Don't try to excuse the offender's behavior, even if it is someone you are really close to.

Don't say, "Lord, please help me to forgive." He is already helping you, and He will be with you all the way through the process. Don't say, "Lord, I want to forgive," because that bypasses the hard choice we have to make. Say, "Lord, I *choose* to forgive."

For every painful memory you have for each person on your list, pray aloud,

> Lord, I choose to forgive (<u>name the person</u>) for (<u>what they did or failed to do</u>), which made me feel (<u>share the painful feelings</u>).

After you have forgiven each person for all the offenses that came to your mind, and after you have honestly expressed how you felt, conclude this step by praying aloud,

> Lord, I choose not to hold on to my resentment. I thank You for setting me free from the bondage of my bitterness. I relinquish my right to seek revenge and ask you to heal my damaged emotions. I now ask You to

bless those who have hurt me. In Jesus' name I pray, amen.

Step 4: Rebellion vs. Submission

We live in a rebellious age. Many people obey laws and authorities only when it is convenient for them. There is a general lack of respect for those in government, and Christians are often as guilty as the rest of society in fostering a critical, rebellious spirit. Certainly, we are not expected to agree with our leaders' policies that are in violation of Scripture, but we are to "honor all people; love the brotherhood, fear God, honor the king" (1 Peter 2:17).

God established all governing authorities, and He requires us to be submissive for our spiritual protection (Romans 13:1-5; 1 Peter 2:13-17). Rebelling against God and His established authority is a very serious sin, and it gives Satan an opportunity to attack. God requires more than just the outward appearance of submission. He wants us to sincerely submit from the heart to those He has placed in authority over us, which is for our spiritual protection.

The Bible makes it clear that we have two main responsibilities toward those in authority over us: to pray for them and to submit to them (Romans 13:1-7; 1 Timothy 2:1-2). To commit yourself to that godly lifestyle, pray the following prayer aloud from your heart:

> *Dear heavenly Father, You have said in the Bible that rebellion is the same thing as witchcraft and that it is as bad as idolatry. I know I have not always been submissive, but instead, I have rebelled in my heart against You and against those You have placed in authority over me. I pray that You would show me all the ways I have been rebellious. I choose now to adopt a submissive spirit and a servant's heart. In Jesus' precious name I pray, amen.*

Being under authority is clearly an act of faith! By submitting, you are trusting God to work through His established lines of authority, even when they are harsh or unkind or tell you to do something you don't want to do. There may be times when those over you abuse their authority and break the laws that are ordained by God for the protection of innocent people. In those cases, you will need to seek help from a *higher* authority for your protection. The laws in your state may require that such abuse be reported to the police or some other governmental agency. If there is continuing abuse (physical, mental, emotional, or sexual) where you live, you may need further counseling help to deal with that situation.

If authorities abuse their position by requiring you to break God's law or compromise your commitment to Him, then you need to obey God rather than man (Acts 4:19-20). Be careful, though. Don't assume that an authority is violating God's Word just because they are telling you to do something you don't like. We all need to adopt a humble, submissive spirit to one another in the fear of Christ (Ephesians 5:21). In addition, however, God has set up specific lines of authority to protect us and give order to our daily lives.

As you prayerfully look over the next list, allow the Lord to show you any *specific* ways in which you have been rebellious to authority. Then, using the prayer of confession that follows the list, specifically confess whatever the Lord brings to your mind.

❑ Civil government (including traffic laws, tax laws, attitude toward government officials) (Romans 13:1-7; 1 Timothy 2:1-4; 1 Peter 2:13-17)

❑ Parents, stepparents, or legal guardians (Ephesians 6:1-3)

❑ Teachers, coaches, school officials (Romans 13:1-4)

❑ Employers, both past and present (1 Peter 2:18-23)

❑ Husband (1 Peter 3:1-4) or wife (Ephesians 5:21; 1 Peter 3:7) [*Note to Husbands:* Take a moment and ask the Lord if your lack of love for your wife could be fostering a rebellious spirit within her. If so, confess that now as a violation of Ephesians 5:22-33.]

❑ Church leaders (Hebrews 13:7)

❑ God (Daniel 9:5,9)

For each way in which the Spirit of God brings to your mind that you have been rebellious, use the following prayer to specifically confess that sin:

> Lord, I confess that I have been rebellious toward (_name_) by (_say what you did specifically_). Thank You for forgiving my rebellion. I choose now to be submissive and obedient to Your Word. By the shed blood of the Lord Jesus Christ, I pray that all ground gained by evil spirits in my life due to my rebellion would be canceled. In Jesus' name I pray, amen.

Step 5: Pride vs. Humility

Pride kills. Pride says, "I don't need God or anyone else's help. I can handle it by myself." Oh no, you can't! We absolutely need God, and we need each other. The apostle Paul wrote that we "worship in the Spirit of God and glory in Christ Jesus and _put no confidence in the flesh_" (Philippians 3:3). That is a good definition of humility: putting no confidence in the flesh, that is, in ourselves—but rather being "strong in the Lord and in the strength of His might" (Ephesians 6:10). Humility is confidence properly placed in God.

Proverbs 3:5-7 expresses a similar thought: "Trust in the LORD with all your heart and do not lean on your own understanding. In all your ways acknowledge Him, and He will make your paths straight. Do not be wise in your own eyes; fear the LORD and turn away from evil." (James 4:6-10 and 1 Peter 5:1-10 also warn us that serious spiritual problems will result when we are proud.) Use the following prayer to express your commitment to living humbly before God:

Dear heavenly Father, You have said that pride goes before destruction and an arrogant spirit before stumbling. I confess that I have been thinking mainly of myself and not others. I have not denied myself, picked up my cross daily, and followed You. As a result, I have given ground to the devil in my life. I have sinned by believing I could be happy and successful on my own. I confess that I have placed my will before Yours and have centered my life around myself instead of You.

I repent of my pride and selfishness and pray that all ground gained in my members by the enemies of the Lord Jesus Christ would be canceled. I choose to rely on the Holy Spirit's power and guidance so I will do nothing from selfishness or empty conceit. With humility of mind, I will regard others as more important than myself. And I choose to make You, Lord, the center of my life.

Please show me now all the specific ways in which I have lived my life in pride. Enable me through love to serve others and in honor to prefer others. I ask all of this in the gentle and humble name of Jesus, my Lord, amen.

(See Proverbs 16:18; Matthew 6:33; 16:24; Romans 12:10; Philippians 2:3.)

Having made that commitment to God in prayer, now allow Him to show you any specific ways in which you have lived in a proud manner. The following list may help you. As the Lord brings to your mind areas of pride, use the prayer that follows to guide you in your confession.

❑ Having a stronger desire to do my will than God's will

❑ Leaning too much on my own understanding and experience rather than seeking God's guidance through prayer and His Word

❑ Relying on my own strengths and abilities instead of depending on the power of the Holy Spirit

❏ Being more concerned about controlling others than about developing self-control

❏ Being too busy doing "important" things to take time to do little things for others

❏ Having a tendency to think that I have no needs

❏ Finding it hard to admit when I am wrong

❏ Being more concerned about pleasing people than pleasing God

❏ Being concerned about getting the credit I feel I deserve

❏ Thinking I am more humble, spiritual, religious, or devoted than others

❏ Being driven to obtain recognition by gaining degrees, titles, or positions

❏ Often feeling that my needs are more important than another person's needs

❏ Considering myself better than others because of my academic, artistic, or athletic abilities and accomplishments

❏ Other ways I have thought more highly of myself than I should (list here):

For each of the above areas that has been true in your life, pray aloud,

> Lord, I agree I have been proud in (name the area). Thank You for forgiving me for my pride. I choose to humble myself before You and others. I choose to place all my confidence in You and none in my flesh. In Jesus' name, amen.

Step 6: Bondage vs. Freedom

Many times we feel trapped in a vicious cycle of "sin-confess-sin-confess" that never seems to end. We can become very discouraged and just give up and give in to the lust of our flesh. To find freedom we must follow James 4:7: "Submit therefore to God. Resist the devil and he will flee from you." We submit to God by confession of sin and repentance (turning away from sin). We resist the devil by rejecting his lies. And we walk in the truth and put on the full armor of God (see Ephesians 6:10-20).

Gaining freedom from sin that has become a habit often requires help from a trusted brother or sister in Christ. James 5:16 says, "Confess your sins to one another and pray for one another so that you may be healed. The effective prayer of a righteous man can accomplish much." Sometimes the assurance of 1 John 1:9 is enough: "If we confess our sins, He is faithful and righteous to forgive us our sins and to cleanse us from all unrighteousness."

Remember, confession is not saying, "I'm sorry"; it is openly admitting, "I did it." Whether you need help from other people or just the accountability of walking in the light before God, pray the following prayer aloud:

> *Dear heavenly Father, You have told me to put on the Lord Jesus Christ and make no provision for the flesh in regard to its lust. I confess that I have given in to fleshly lusts that wage war against my soul. I thank You that in Christ my sins are already forgiven, but I have broken Your holy law and given the devil a chance to wage war in my members. I come to You now to confess and renounce these sins of the flesh so that I might be cleansed and set free from the bondage of sin. Please reveal to my mind all the sins of the flesh I have committed and the ways I have grieved the Holy Spirit. In Jesus' holy name I pray, amen.*

(See Proverbs 28:13 NIV; Romans 6:12-13; 13:14; 2 Corinthians 4:2; James 4:1; 1 Peter 2:11; 5:8.)

The following list contains many sins of the flesh. A prayerful examination of Mark 7:20-23, Galatians 5:19-21, Ephesians 4:25-31, and other Scripture passages will help you to be even more thorough. Look over the list below and the Scriptures just listed and ask the Holy Spirit to bring to your mind the sins you need to confess. He may reveal others to you as well. For each one the Lord shows you, pray a prayer of confession from your heart. There is a sample prayer following the list. (*Note:* Sexual sins, divorce, eating disorders, substance abuse, abortion, suicidal tendencies, and perfectionism will be dealt with later in this step. Further counseling help may be necessary to find complete healing and freedom in these and other areas.)

- ❏ Stealing
- ❏ Quarreling or fighting
- ❏ Jealousy or envy
- ❏ Complaining or criticism
- ❏ Sarcasm
- ❏ Lustful actions
- ❏ Gossip or slander
- ❏ Swearing
- ❏ Apathy or laziness
- ❏ Lying
- ❏ Hatred
- ❏ Anger
- ❏ Lustful thoughts
- ❏ Drunkenness
- ❏ Cheating
- ❏ Procrastination
- ❏ Greed or materialism
- ❏ Others:

> *Lord, I confess that I have committed the sin of (name the sins). Thank You for Your forgiveness and cleansing. I now turn away from these sins and turn to You, Lord. Strengthen me by Your Holy Spirit to obey You. In Jesus' name, amen.*

Wrong Sexual Use of Our Body

It is our responsibility not to allow sin to reign (rule) in our mortal bodies. We accomplish this by not using our bodies or another person's body as instruments of unrighteousness (see Romans 6:12-13). Sexual immorality is not only a sin against God but is a sin against your body, the temple of the Holy Spirit (1 Corinthians 6:18-19). To find freedom from sexual bondage, begin by praying the following prayer:

> *Lord, I ask You to bring to my mind every sexual use of my body as an instrument of unrighteousness so that I can renounce these sexual sins and break their bondage in Christ. In Jesus' name I pray, amen.*

As the Lord brings to your mind every wrong sexual use of your body, whether it was done to you (rape, incest, sexual molestation) or willingly by you (pornography, masturbation, sexual immorality), renounce *every* occasion:

> *Lord, I renounce (name the specific use of your body) with (name any other person involved). I ask You to break that sinful and emotional bond with (name).*

After you are finished, commit your body to the Lord by praying,

> *Lord, I renounce all these uses of my body as an instrument of unrighteousness, and I admit to any willful participation. I choose now to present my eyes, mouth, mind, heart, hands, feet, and sexual organs to You as instruments of righteousness. I present my whole body to You as a living sacrifice, holy and acceptable. I*

choose to reserve the sexual use of my body for marriage only.

I reject the devil's lie that my body is not clean or that it is dirty or in any way unacceptable to You as a result of my past sexual experiences. Lord, thank You that You have totally cleansed and forgiven me and that You love and accept me just the way I am. Therefore, I choose now to accept myself and my body as clean in Your eyes. In Jesus' name, amen.

Special Prayers for Special Needs

Divorce

Lord, I confess to You any part that I played in my divorce (ask the Lord to show you specifics). Thank You for Your forgiveness, and I choose not to condemn myself. I renounce the lie that divorce affects my identity in Christ. I am a child of God, and I reject the lie that I am a second-class Christian because of the divorce. I reject the lie that says I am worthless, unlovable, and that my life is empty and meaningless. I am complete in Christ, who loves me and accepts me just as I am. Lord, I commit the healing of all hurts in my life to You, as I have chosen to forgive those who have hurt me. I also place my future into Your hands and choose to seek human companionship in Your church. I surrender to Your will in regard to another spouse. I pray all this in the healing name of Jesus, my Savior, Lord, and closest friend, amen.

Homosexuality

Lord, I renounce the lie that You have created me or anyone else to be homosexual, and I agree that in Your Word You clearly forbid homosexual behavior. I choose to accept myself as a child of God, and I thank You that You created me as a man (woman). I renounce all homosexual thoughts, urges, drives, and acts, and I renounce all ways that Satan has used these things to pervert my relationships. I announce that I am free in Christ to relate to the opposite sex and my own sex in the way that You intended. In Jesus' name, amen.

Abortion

Lord, I confess that I was not a proper guardian and keeper of the life You entrusted to me, and I admit that as sin. Thank You that because of Your forgiveness, I can forgive myself. I recognize the child is in Your caring hands for all eternity. In Jesus' name, amen.

Suicidal Tendencies

Lord, I renounce all suicidal thoughts and any attempts I've made to take my own life or in any way injure myself. I renounce the lie that life is hopeless and that I can find peace and freedom by taking my own life. Satan is a thief who comes to steal, kill, and destroy. I choose life in Christ, who said He came to give me life and give it abundantly. Thank You for Your forgiveness that allows me to forgive myself. I choose to believe that there is always hope in Christ. In Jesus' name I pray, amen.

Drivenness and Perfectionism

Lord, I renounce the lie that my self-worth is dependent upon my ability to perform. I announce the truth that my identity and sense of worth are found in who I am as Your child. I renounce seeking the approval and acceptance of other people, and I choose to believe that I am already approved and accepted in Christ because of His death and resurrection for me. I choose to believe the truth that I have been saved, not by deeds done in righteousness, but according to Your mercy. I choose to believe that I am no longer under the curse of the law because Christ became a curse for me. I receive the free gift of life in Christ and choose to abide in Him. I renounce striving for perfection by living under the law.

By Your grace, heavenly Father, I choose from this day forward to walk by faith in the power of Your Holy Spirit according to what You have said is true. In Jesus' name, amen.

Eating Disorders or Self-Mutilation

Lord, I renounce the lie that my value as a person is dependent upon my appearance or my performance. I renounce cutting or abusing myself, vomiting, using laxatives, or starving myself as a means of being in control, altering my appearance, or trying to cleanse myself of evil. I announce that only the blood of the Lord Jesus cleanses me from sin. I realize that I have been bought with a price and that my body, the temple of the Holy Spirit, belongs to God. Therefore, I choose to glorify God in my body. I renounce the lie that I am evil or that any part of my body is evil. Thank You that You accept me just the way I am in Christ. In Jesus' name I pray, amen.

Substance Abuse

Lord, I confess that I have misused substances (alcohol, tobacco, food, prescription or street drugs) for the purpose of pleasure, to escape reality, or to cope with difficult problems. I confess that I have abused my body and programmed my mind in a harmful way. I have quenched the Holy Spirit as well. Thank You for forgiving me. I renounce any satanic connection or influence in my life through my misuse of food or chemicals. I cast my anxieties onto Christ, who loves me. I commit myself to yield no longer to substance abuse—instead I choose to allow the Holy Spirit to direct and empower me. In Jesus' name, amen.

Step 7: Curses vs. Blessings

The next step to freedom is to renounce the sins of your ancestors as well as any satanic assignments directed toward you or your ministry. According to the Ten Commandments, iniquities can be passed on from one generation to the next if you don't renounce the sins of your ancestors and claim your new spiritual heritage in Christ. You are not guilty for the sin of any ancestor, but because of their sin, you may be genetically predisposed to certain strengths or weaknesses and influenced by the physical and spiritual atmosphere in which you were raised. These conditions can contribute toward causing you to struggle with a particular sin. Ask the Lord to show you specifically what sins are characteristic of your family by praying the following prayer:

> *Dear heavenly Father, I ask You to reveal to my mind now all the sins of my ancestors that are being passed down through family lines. I want to be free from those influences and walk in my new identity as a child of God. In Jesus' name, amen.*

As the Lord brings those areas of family sin to your mind, list them below. You will be specifically renouncing them later in this step.

In order to walk free from the sins of your ancestors and any assignments targeted against you, read the following declaration and pray the following prayer aloud. Remember, you have all the authority and protection you need in Christ to take your stand against Satan and his demons.

Declaration

> I here and now reject and disown all the sins of my ancestors. I specifically renounce the sins of (<u>name the areas of family sin the Lord revealed to you</u>). As one who has now been delivered from the domain of darkness into the kingdom of God's Son, I choose to believe that all the sins and iniquities of my ancestors have been confessed and that I now stand forgiven and cleansed in Christ.
>
> As one who has been crucified and raised with Jesus Christ and who sits with Him in heavenly places, I renounce all satanic assignments that are directed toward me and my ministry. I choose to believe that Jesus has broken every curse that Satan and his workers have put on me. I announce to Satan and all his forces that Christ became a curse for me when He died for my sins on the cross. I reject any and every way in which Satan may claim ownership of me. I belong to the Lord Jesus Christ, who purchased me with His own blood. I reject all blood sacrifices whereby Satan may claim ownership of me. I declare myself to be fully and eternally signed over and committed to the Lord Jesus Christ. By the authority I have in Christ, I now command every enemy of the Lord Jesus to leave my presence. I commit myself to my heavenly Father to do His will from this day forward.

Prayer

> Dear heavenly Father, I come to You as Your child, bought out of slavery to sin by the blood of the Lord Jesus Christ. You are the Lord of the universe and the Lord of my life. I submit my body to You as an instrument of righteousness, a living and holy sacrifice, that I may glorify You in my body. I now ask You to fill me with the Holy Spirit. I commit myself to the renewing of my mind in order to prove that Your will is good, acceptable, and perfect for me. All this I pray in the name and authority of the risen Lord Jesus Christ, amen.

Your Identity

Your identity and sense of worth come from knowing who you are in Christ. Your need to be *accepted*, *secure*, and *significant* can only be fully realized in your eternal relationship with God. As a final exercise, let me encourage you to meditate on the following truths from my book *Who I Am in Christ*. Read the entire list out loud until you are convinced that you indeed are God's child and that He will meet all your needs according to His riches in glory:

In Christ

I am God's child (John 1:12)

I am Christ's friend (John 15:5)

I have been justified (Romans 5:1)

I am united with the Lord, and I am one spirit with Him (1 Corinthians 6:17)

I have been bought with a price: I belong to God (1 Corinthians 6:19-20)

I am a member of Christ's body (1 Corinthians 12:27)

I am a saint, a holy one (Ephesians 1:1)

I have been adopted as God's child (Ephesians 1:5)

I have direct access to God through the Holy Spirit (Ephesians 2:18)

I have been redeemed and forgiven of all my sins (Colossians 1:14)

I am complete in Christ (Colossians 2:10)

I renounce the lie that I am guilty, unprotected, alone, or abandoned, because in Christ I am totally secure. God says...

I am free from condemnation (Romans 8:1-2)

I am assured that all things work together for good (Romans 8:28)

I am free from any condemning charges against me (Romans 8:31-34)

I cannot be separated from the love of God (Romans 8:35-39)

I have been established, anointed, and sealed by God (2 Corinthians 1:21-22)

I am confident that the good work God has begun in me will be perfected (Philippians 1:6)

I am a citizen of heaven (Philippians 3:20)

I am hidden with Christ in God (Colossians 3:3)

I have not been given a spirit of fear, but of power, love, and a sound mind (2 Timothy 1:7)

I can find grace and mercy to help in time of need (Hebrews 4:16)

I am born of God and the evil one cannot touch me (1 John 5:18)

I renounce the lie that I am worthless, inadequate, helpless, or hopeless, because in Christ I am deeply significant. God says…

I am the salt of the earth and the light of the world (Matthew 5:13-14)

I am a branch of the true vine, Jesus, a channel of His life (John 15:1,5)

I have been chosen and appointed by God to bear fruit (John 15:16)

I am a personal, Spirit-empowered witness of Christ's (Acts 1:8)

I am a temple of God (1 Corinthians 3:16)

I am a minister of reconciliation for God (2 Corinthians 5:17-21)

I am God's co-worker (2 Corinthians 6:1)

I am seated with Christ in the heavenly realm (Ephesians 2:6)

I am God's workmanship, created for good works (Ephesians 2:10)

I may approach God with freedom and confidence (Ephesians 3:12)

I can do all things through Christ who strengthens me! (Philippians 4:13)[6]

1. *The Steps to Freedom in Christ* can be purchased in separate book form at any Christian bookstore or from Freedom in Christ Ministries. The Steps are also contained in my book *The Bondage Breaker* (Harvest House, 2000). For a detailed discussion of how to help others in this way, see my book *Discipleship Counseling* (Regal Books, 2003).

2. After our Living Free in Christ conferences, we offer personal appointments for those who can't get through the Steps in a group setting but can with the help of a mature encourager. These Christians are given an extended appointment that can last for several hours, depending upon the degree of difficulty of their conflicts and their knowledge of God and His ways.

   At one conference, a pretest was given to counselees before the appointment. Then another one was given three months later. The results from this conference showed remarkable improvement in a number of areas: 57 percent in depression, 54 percent in anxiety, 49 percent in fear, 55 percent in anger, 50 percent in tormenting thoughts, 53 percent in negative habits, and 56 percent in self-esteem. For further research results, testimonies accompanied by explanation, and instruction for how this methodology can be used in Christian counseling, see Neil T. Anderson, Fernando Garzon, and Judy King, *Released from Bondage* (Nashville, TN: Thomas Nelson Publishers, 2002).

3. John R.W. Stott, *Tyndale New Testament Commentaries: The Epistles of John* (Grand Rapids, MI: Wm. B. Eerdmans Publishing Company, 1964), p. 189. Stott further comments, "It may be objected, if the sin unto death is the blasphemy against the Holy Spirit committed by a hardened unbeliever, how can John call him a brother? To be exact, he does not. It is the one whose sin is 'not unto death' who is termed a brother; he whose sin is 'unto death' is neither named or described" (p. 189).

   In regard to the phrase "God will for him give life" (verse 16), Stott observes, "Since God is the giver of life, and since usually asking is man's part and giving God's, some have suggested a change of subject in the middle of this sentence, so that the second *he* refers to God, and not the intercessor. So RV, RSV. But the verbs are so simply and closely coupled in the Greek, that a different subject would be forced. It is better to accept the ascription of real efficacy to prayer (as in verse 15), so that, under God, he who asks for a man may be said not just to gain it for him but to give it to him. In either case the *him* to whom life is given is the sinner, not the intercessor" (p. 190).

4. Theodore H. Epp, *Praying with Authority* (Lincoln, NE: Back to the Bible Broadcast, 1965), p. 93.

5. This condensed version of the Steps to Freedom in Christ is taken from Neil T. Anderson, *Living Free in Christ* (Ventura, CA: Gospel Light Publications, 1995). © 1995 by Gospel Light/ Regal Books, Ventura, CA 93003. Used by Permission. For an expanded version of the Steps, see note 1.

6. Adapted from Neil T. Anderson, *Who I Am in Christ* (Ventura, CA: Gospel Light Publications, 2001). © 2001 by Gospel Light/Regal Books, Ventura, CA 93003. Used by Permission.

The Bondage Breaker® Series

In each book of this new series, bestselling author Neil Anderson takes you to the Word of God and digs out truth that will bring you freedom in your life. As you allow your mind to be renewed by the Scripture in key areas of understanding, you'll gain confidence in your identity as a beloved child of God—and you'll walk free in Jesus Christ!

Praying by the Power of the Spirit

"If prayer is so important, why is it so difficult?" Starting from this basic question nearly all of us have asked, Neil Anderson explores biblical, practical ways we can intimately connect with our loving heavenly Father, looking at—

- what role giving thanks has in prayer
- how we can confidently expose our spiritual and emotional struggles before God
- how prayer can release us from spiritual bondage and help us walk in the Spirit
- how personal, two-way dialogue with the Father can direct us in interceding for others
- the gracious way God leads us to love Him, not His blessings

Finding God's Will in Spiritually Deceptive Times

Who has the authority to speak for God? How do we hear His message? Does it come through other people, through the Scriptures, or both? These are questions that nearly every Christian has struggled with.

According to Neil Anderson, the answers must be based on two powerful truths: We are alive in Christ, and we are God's children. From this foundation, he goes on to examine

- how we can identify counterfeit messages
- what the roles of the Scripture, the Holy Spirit, and other believers are in helping us find God's will
- the ways in which we need to be alert to Satan's deceptions
- how we can replace fear of making the wrong decision with freedom
- what true spiritual discernment is and how to exercise it